DEEPER INTO JOHN'S GOSPEL

By Arthur Fay Sueltz

Deeper Into John's Gospel
New Directions from The Ten Commandments
When the Wood Is Green

Deeper Into John's Gospel

ARTHUR FAY SUELTZ

Published in San Francisco by

HARPER & ROW, PUBLISHERS

New York, Hagerstown

San Francisco, London

Acknowledgment is made for permission to reprint from *The New English Bible*, © The Delegates of the Oxford University Press and the Syndics of the Cambridge University Press, 1961, 1970.

DEEPER INTO JOHN'S GOSPEL. Copyright © 1979 by Arthur Fay Sueltz. All rights reserved. Printed in the United States of America. No part of this book may be used or reproduced in any manner whatsoever without written permission except in the case of brief quotations embodied in critical articles and reviews. For information address Harper & Row, Publishers, Inc., 10 East 53rd Street, New York, NY 10022. Published simultaneously in Canada by Fitzhenry & Whiteside Limited, Toronto.

FIRST EDITION

Designed by Jim Mennick

Library of Congress Cataloging in Publication Data

Sueltz, Arthur Fay.
   DEEPER INTO JOHN'S GOSPEL.

   1. Bible. N.T. John—Criticism, interpretation, etc. I. Title.
BS2615.S8 1979   226'.5'07   783353
ISBN 0-06-067764-3

79 80 81 82 83 10 9 8 7 6 5 4 3 2 1

Contents

*Questions for Reflection and Discussion
are found at the end of each chapter*

530

Preface

In Peter Benchley's novel *The Deep,* a suspense story about sunken treasure, three men aboard a cabin cruiser are searching for Spanish gold. Benchley writes that one of them "contemplated the possible perils and as usual found himself ambivalent toward them, nervous but excited, afraid of the unknown but impatient to meet it, eager to do things he had never done. As he looked at the dark water a shiver of anticipation made the hair on his arms rise."

I feel something of that shiver of anticipation when I open John's Gospel. Who knows what might lie beneath the surface of the story? We might hear the sound of a voice not our own. If we did, what would such a voice say? What would we do? Would tomorrow be just like today?

People of faith keep saying they hear such a voice speaking from deep within John's Gospel. All kinds of people have helped me listen for it. I have soaked up their insights like a boy discovering a new neighborhood. Because of them, I have heard words I had not heard before, words I have made my own. I want to give credit to everyone who has helped me hear that voice more clearly.

But often today I can't tell where their perception of what that voice says leaves off and mine begins. Join me in listening for the sound of the voice that speaks from within John's story.

DEEPER INTO JOHN'S GOSPEL

1. Any Good Word?
(John 1:1–3*)

A word sends one man to prison and sets another man free. Such words become events. I remember an artist in Maine who gathered people together every evening and described the sunset. When he had to leave the community the people said, "But you *can't* leave. We never had sunsets before you came." Somehow at a word the event had come alive.

Some people claim that they want deeds, not words, and I know what they mean. I have a feeling, though, that the people who wrote the Bible would never have understood the request. For them words were deeds. They saw a spoken word as the most creative thing in existence.

Yet their interest lay not simply in the Word they heard. They wanted to know the one who spoke, as I do. After all, I married my wife, not the words she speaks, though I would not have known her if she had never spoken to me. Facts are nothing without interpretation.

When I pick up the Gospel of John and start to read, I find it a haunting and mysterious book, yet a book so simply written that children enjoy it. Most people understand the surface details of the story John tells, but beneath the surface almost every sentence bursts with hints and allusions.

---

* I suggest that the passage from John which I discuss in each chapter be read before reading my comments.

This book speaks to me in a voice not my own—a voice beyond even that of John. What I hear does not clear up all the ambiguities of life, nor does it unveil the one who speaks. Even John doesn't try to explain it all, or ask me to understand and analyze all he writes. He leaves the unsayable unsaid but urges me to listen for the voice he hears.

John begins at the beginning: "When all things began. . . ."* Right at the start he plunges me into the mystery of the Garden of Eden and leads me from there to the Garden of Gethsemane. What a surprise! I find myself walking from the place where Adam hid to the place where Jesus prayed. Along the way John keeps asking me to listen for the word that comes to me where I try to either hide or pray. I do seem to live somewhere between Eden and Gethsemane—between hiding and praying.

And as I listen, I begin to hear a word that goes beyond good advice. It's a word that may not solve all my problems, but in which I catch the sound of wonder and glory I have not heard before. A glorious word sounding above the fury of life on earth, it's the word I have waited to hear. And John heard it too. No wonder he writes, "When all things began, the Word already was. The Word dwelt with God, and what God was, the Word was . . . and through him all things came to be."

As a child I once wondered if God ever felt lonely when nothing else existed. God and nothing, nothing, nothing. Now suddenly I hear that at the beginning God had with him the Word, and I catch the sound of something I had missed. I know what it feels like to have a word inside of me. A word saying, Art, write a letter, or Art, paint a picture, or Art, go out and sail your boat. It's just a word,

---

* Biblical quotations in this book are from The New English Bible, unless noted otherwise. In some cases, however, I paraphrase the Bible rather than quote it directly.

but all at once I'm not alone. And having such a word within me begins to make things happen.

John writes as if he believes that, because God had such a word within himself, creation began. Creation came slowly at first, perhaps, but eventually there were oak trees and carrots, salmon and elephants, ladybugs and cows. Then off in a corner where life grew a little faster, God carefully brought into being a new creature. He created someone he could relate to in a personal way; someone to talk with, to work with; someone to do creative things with; someone to know person to person.

Very soon, however, the people who walked and talked with God in the Garden of Eden heard other words. One word led to another, until people stopped listening for the one Word that sustains life. Then anxiety and shame began to break them down and rip them up. I get the feeling that God has been up against this ever since. With John, I see all human history as a great agonizing attempt on God's part to get people to listen to him again.

Many people do try. Some of my friends listen for God's voice in creation, in nature. And they tell me they hear it in the beauty of a sunset, or a waterfall, or even the silence of the mountains. Such experiences *can* tell me something of God; but when you throw in cholera and cancer, what does nature sound like then?

Other people tell me we all have a divine spark flickering in us. We can speak simply and directly to God, who is like our brother or sister. Splendid! But I need more than someone simply like me; I need more than a brother with me. I need someone almighty who can reach down and get me out of real jams.

So I listen for that unreasonable, often irrational and contradictory voice I've begun to hear behind the words of John, who writes, "The Word became flesh; he came to dwell among us, and we saw his glory, such glory as befits the Father's only Son, full of grace and truth" (1:14). John does not ask me to explain or understand that. He *does* ask me to believe that God Almighty comes close to me when I need him most.

Some people talk about a simple Gospel. I don't believe that such a thing exists. What artist has ever captured all he saw, or what musician all he heard? And who has ever truly known the mind of God? Still I never really hear a word until it lives for me.

Most of the great things in life have no tangible existence. Justice for instance. In exasperation a person protests, "There ain't no justice," and he's right. I can't touch justice, or mercy, or love. They exist in the abstract, and we use what words we have to try to describe and interpret them.

All through history poets and prophets have used every word they could think of to get people to listen to God's Word. At best, they themselves heard only a fragment of it. And the people they spoke to often misunderstood completely. Which simply means that what God has to say goes far beyond the power of human speech.

No wonder late one night God walked down the stairs of heaven with a baby in his arms. "The Word became flesh." People—individual persons—influence me much more than do the abstractions of life. William James once said that he could not define goodness, but he could point to a good person. He could understand goodness when he saw it in the flesh. There the word *goodness* came alive for him, and he heard it.

Behind the words of John I hear a voice telling me that God spelled himself out in the language of life in that stranger from Galilee. That strange Galilean who did the strangest things in the strangest ways. In Jesus of Nazareth I catch a glimpse of what lies behind and beyond and within and through all of life. God took an undiluted dose of humanity. He knows firsthand what it will take to salvage us. That does something for my understanding of God and my appreciation of Jesus.

One summer night in Michigan a young mother tucked

her small daughter into bed, while outside the lightning flashed, and thunder shook the house. After she finally got her daughter settled, the mother went downstairs and tried to read in the living room, but the storm kept up. Her daughter lay in bed as long as she could, but finally she jumped out of bed, ran downstairs, and threw herself into her mother's arms, saying, "Mommy, I'm scared." Her mother held and comforted her; then the two of them walked upstairs again. She said, "Remember, honey, God loves you and he'll take care of you and keep you safe."

The mother went back downstairs into the living room and made herself comfortable. In about five minutes there stood the little girl again at the foot of the stairs: "Mommy, I'm still afraid."

And the mother said encouragingly, "Honey, I've told you that you have to get your sleep. You're perfectly safe. God loves you and he'll take care of you."

"I know God loves me," answered her daughter. "But, Mommy, when it's thundering and lightning outside, I want someone with skin on to love me."

Jesus was born for this, that God's Word might live. God is not abstract, nor is he simply the small and human baby Jesus. God enters personally into life, for the ultimate things of human life are personal; it is this that John means to convey.

What then does this event have to say to me as I struggle with my viruses and my taxes and my own private neuroses? What kind of word does God have for people caught in tangled and complex situations?

The word I hear allows me to order my life by reality, by things as they really are. That's quite different from the words of a puritanical legalist who, shaking his finger at a man caught in an affair, tells him, "This has got to stop. Break it off once and for all; it's sin."

"But that will hurt several people beyond repair," the man responds. "Must I never see her again?"

Such a break might be a safe course, yet a selfish one,

for the man's own soul. He needs a word to help him see things as they really are. Because the situation he created involves him in some responsibilities, he may have to do something much harder than simply break it off.

Heavy-handed moralism may cause him to break off an affair that's wrong, but such moralism doesn't go deep enough. What can it do to untangle all of the man's mixed-up emotions? He just doesn't yet have it within himself to be the kind of person he wants to be. Instinctively he knows that something has to happen deep within himself before he can arrive at a good solution.

He needs more than a pat answer, more than an infallible moral rule. He needs, first, a willingness to offer himself and his situation as completely as he can to as much of the Word of God as he hears in Christ. If he does this, he may recognize that God has already gone to work in his life by disturbing him and calling him to attention.

At that point, he will probably see that he has to talk things over with the woman involved. The kind of talk that will allow her to hear the truth he has heard—that will allow her to be drawn into a deeper encounter with God, if she herself permits it. God always has another move to make, beginning where we are. The whole situation may be redeemed if one person allows God to come in at one corner of it.

We don't need people to wag their fingers at us and moralize, beating us over the head with their Bibles. We do need people like the person who wrote this Gospel to help us face reality as it is. From there we can move to straightforwardly asking God to come in on the jam we're in. When legalism and moralism become judgmental, Jesus says, "Nor do I condemn you. You may go; do not sin again" (8:11).

No wonder John goes on to say, "And we saw his glory, such glory as befits the Father's only Son, full of grace and truth." Frankly, I hadn't thought much about glory. What does the word mean anyway? It's almost impossible to define, not because it means so little but because it means so much. I suppose we use glory to describe something we can't otherwise put into words.

People need some glory in their lives, and they will have it. We all need something to sing about, something to celebrate. John's Gospel, so completely human that it contains both Judas and Jesus, comes packed with glory, as does the whole Bible. Anything that ever made a person's heart beat faster or blood flow hotter, I find here. The glory of political power, the glory of great temples, the glory of towering mountains, the glory of the sunrise and the sunset, the glory of the stars, the glory of a woman's hair, the glory of white lilies, the glory of youth, the glory of old age. But nothing comes with quite the force of "We saw his glory, such glory as befits the Father's only Son."

The glory of Jesus. What is it? John believed he knew; he believed he had seen it. I think he saw it outside the city wall as he stood in the shadow of the cross. Who could ever forget that? And the sound of the hammer echoing across the valley, or the soldier's spear going into the side of Jesus. "And we saw his glory. . . ." Who can understand such a mystery? Of what use is a God who dies like that? A harmless, helpless, unarmed God who will not make people believe him or obey him.

Since the beginning he has never seemed like much of a God at all to many people. He does not strut around as the supreme egotist of the world. Nor does he act as I expect him to act and damn my enemies to the hell they seem so richly to deserve.

This Jesus looks just as helpless today as he ever did. Around him I see a ragged rabble of a church that sings hosanna on Sunday then runs for its life from the garden on Friday. We make great protestations of faith, like Peter, and then betray Jesus. We argue among ourselves about who should be greatest in the kingdom and do not think to wash his feet. Jesus with this poor crowd of wretched preachers like myself. I who proclaim the Gospel and hardly live it. I who talk about the love of God and have difficulty appearing friendly.

In exactly such circumstances John said, "we saw his glory, such glory as befits the Father's only Son." I can't explain that. But looking at that "foolishness," I do catch a glimpse of the glory. And that's a good word.

QUESTIONS FOR REFLECTION AND DISCUSSION

1. How has your understanding of God changed in the last ten years? (If you're meeting with a group of people for the first time, you might introduce yourselves to each other by answering this question in turn.)
2. In what sense, if any, do words make things happen in your life?
3. What do you think of the idea that, in Jesus, "God took an undiluted dose of humanity"? If you agree, what difference does it make to you?
4. Do you think God has another move to make in your life?
5. How can you distinguish between your own intuition and any word God might speak within you?

2. The Dark and Light of It (1:4–5)

I remember standing deep in the bowels of the Crystal Caves in Oregon with my wife and two small children, when the guide turned out the light, plunging us into sudden and total darkness. Not a flicker of light anywhere. I didn't move, nor did I want to. Besides, I had no idea which direction to take. All kinds of things could happen if I moved in the darkness. I might lose touch with my wife, lose the children, or get lost myself.

Isn't that exactly how a lot of us feel every now and then—as if we're in the dark? So many things demand immediate and specific answers. A young wife wipes a tear from her eye and asks, "Am I sexually dead at twenty-seven?" A college senior mutters that he doesn't have the strength to stand up to his father.

When you feel that you're in the dark, how do you get your bearings? How do you know what direction to take in life?

Albert Schweizer gave up a great academic career. He had no interest in a dream house in the suburbs but plunged instead into the African bush, helping sick people. Did he take the right direction? Or did J. Paul Getty, with his massive fortune and art collection and his mansion, Sutton Place, set in a thousand acres of rolling hills bordered by trees and well-manicured hedges?

Dizzy Dean will never go down as one of the great

theologians of the twentieth century. But he could throw a baseball like few others, and he gave us his own brand of grammar. Hoover Rupert, a prominent American minister, recalls reading in the *Baseball Digest* of the day when Dizzy Dean, talking to a reporter, called Howard Ehmke, a Philadelphia Athletics pitcher, a "fiddle hitcher." Immediately the reporter asked Dean what he meant.

"Well now," said Dean, "a fiddle hitcher is a guy who has been up in the major leagues a long time and has lost his stuff. So he takes to fiddle hitching to get the batters out. He's a guy who fiddles around, hitching up his trousers, pulling at his cap, kicking at the dirt, anything to get the batter riled."

I know what Dizzy Dean meant, because I've run into people like that in life—people so unsure of themselves that they try to psyche me out. We start discussing some subject about which such a person knows nothing, and he pulls a quote out of the air and longwindedly makes my ideas on the subject look terrible in comparison. Or he makes me so mad that I explode, walk off, and leave him king of the hill.

I've seen people who, their faith wearing thin, seem to grope for direction in life. They find themselves in a spot they could have handled easily fifteen years ago. But now, as Dizzy Dean would say, they've lost their stuff. They start to fiddle hitch. It works for a while, until all of a sudden everybody *knows* they've lost their stuff, and a series of hits knocks them out of the box.

To all of us who have ever felt in the dark, the writer of John's Gospel says of Jesus, "All that came to be was alive with his life, and that life was the light of men. The light shines on in the dark, and the darkness has never mastered it."

John writes like a man who had seen a flash of lightning light up an otherwise dark scene. In an instant he saw his whole world ablaze with light—he had seen Jesus! He could not keep something like that to himself.

Compare John's attitude with that of the patriarch in the apocryphal story of Khrushchev and Titov, the Russian cosmonaut. After the cosmonaut landed, Khrushchev is said to have asked him if he had seen anyone in space during his journey, to which Titov replied, "Yes, I saw God out there."

"I knew he was there," Khrushchev answered, "but you know our policy, so don't tell anybody."

Not long afterward, Titov had an interview with the patriarch of the Russian church. This Christian leader asked the cosmonaut if he had seen God out in space. This time Titov, remembering Khrushchev's warning, said, "No, I didn't see God out there." To which the patriarch replied, "I knew it. I knew God was dead. But you know our policy, so please don't tell anybody."

How totally different John's statement: "The light shines on in the dark, and the darkness has never mastered it."

All kinds of light shine in our world. Every morning the sun brings the world back to life; houses and trees and people and flowers begin to take on the shape and color that the darkness had drained out of them. In the light of the sun, I can see where I am. I can look at my situation and opportunities and begin to see where I might go.

We also have the light of the moon at night, though it is not as strong as the sun and often hidden by a passing cloud. Yet on a clear night in the light of the full moon, the earth takes on an unearthly beauty.

Besides this natural light we have artificial light. We can light up our homes and our cities at midnight almost as brightly as at midday, disregarding our need to conserve.

But the word *light* also has a deeper meaning. Another kind of light shines in our world. You find yourself at a party you hadn't really wanted to come to. You had expected a lot of awful people to show up, but it hasn't turned out to be as bad as you expected. Not everybody talks business or baseball.

Then all of a sudden the doorbell rings. A man and a woman come into the room and are introduced. You're not sure you like them, but then maybe you're not sure you like anybody you haven't met before. After a brief flurry of trivial talk, you begin to feel something different. From the minute these two new people come into the room, everybody seems to light up—to come to life.

On a different level, I remember taking trigonometry in high school—or, worse yet, having trigonomety take me. For a whole semester I couldn't make the equations work properly. In fact, nothing worked for me in the course. I hated it. I dreaded going to class.

I did so badly that I had to take the class over again, but this time from a different teacher—a teacher who knew the difference between teaching mathematics and teaching people. And it felt as if someone had turned on the light. I began not only to understand the equations but to enjoy them. They made sense to me.

When John's Gospel talks about Jesus as the light of life it means something like that. What Jesus did, what he said, lit up people's lives. Everyone he touched seemed more alive afterward.

A lot of the people Jesus came into contact with felt in the dark about God. And to people who felt that way he kept saying such things as, God knows you. He cares about how your life gets lived. Take hold of yourself and start living as if you believed it.

Soon people began to believe they heard God speaking to them through Jesus. That sheds a lot of light on my understanding of where I can look for God today. Not out in space somewhere but incarnate—in the flesh. "If a man says, 'I love God,' while hating his brother, he is a liar. If he does not love the brother whom he has seen, it cannot be that he loves God whom he has not seen" (1 John 4:20).

Someone asked him, "Lord, when was it that we saw you hungry and fed you, or thirsty and gave you drink?

. . . When did we see you ill or in prison, and come to visit you?" Jesus answered, "I tell you this: anything you did for one of my brothers here, however humble, you did for me" (Matt. 25:37–40).

Surprisingly, I discover that the light of God falls upon me through the lives of such people. I can discover the light of God's presence in the person who lives closest to me. That person may not agree with me; I may not always have nice warm feelings for him. Yet God comes to me in the person who needs me the most.

The late British Methodist preacher W. Edwin Sangester once told his congregation about an experience he and his family had during the Nazi blitzkrieg. When bombs destroyed his home during an air-raid, he and his family moved into an air-raid shelter along with hundreds of other similarly homeless people. The desolate, suspicious band huddled together in a crowded shelter.

The first night they had nothing to drink—no water and no tea—so early the next morning Sangester went back to the wreckage of his house and searched for the precious reserve of tea and sugar which, by government order, had been put there against a time of need. Finding the reserve, he brought it to the shelter, thinking to use it for his family.

However, in one extravagant gesture, he brewed a great tub of tea—enough for just one cup for each of the entire crowd of forced neighbors. It looked like a stupid waste of the tea that could have served his family for many days to come, yet it changed the atmosphere of the whole shelter. The darkness of bitterness and suspicion seemed to melt away. Other people brought out their carefully hoarded reserves and shared them.

The spirit of that shelter changed so much that the government heard about it and sent a representative to find out its secret. They wanted to reproduce that spirit in other shelters as well! That's the kind of light that God lets loose in the flesh.

It's also the kind of light that helps you when you're in

the dark about your personal failures. I know of a county probation officer who works with juveniles. He tells of a preteenager who found himself involved in involuntary manslaughter as a small child. As he grew up, he carried a terrible load of guilt, and he privately hoped someone would punish him enough to remove that guilt. He became depressed—so much so that he had to find some relief.

He got some drugs and stole a car so that the police would finally arrest him. Some time later, in his own way, he poured out his story to the probation officer. When the young man had finally finished, the officer said to him, "You know, just because you made a mistake doesn't mean *you* are a mistake." Suddenly the light of God shone through the life of a probation officer into the darkness of a young man's depression and guilt.

John said, "the light shines on in the dark, and the darkness has never mastered it." It survived the darkness of ignorance that settled over Europe from the fourth century to the ninth. Why? Because here and there people of faith kept the light alive, though it was dim at times.

Nor did the darkness of wealth and affluence and power that drenched the church of Europe in the thirteenth century put out the light. The church almost forgot what it stood for, but in the darkness a little Italian went around singing about the Lord Jesus. He gave away everything that he had, and yet he owned everything. And thousands of men and women began to see the light burning in Francis of Assisi.

In the eighteenth century, the established church of England lapsed into a kind of darkness. But John Wesley road up and down the country, and wherever he rode, light shone.

In our own secular, materialistic, violent, cynical day, suddenly and surprisingly the light of Jesus Christ appears. It shows up in music for instance, and not just in so-called sacred music but in musicals like *Godspell* and *Jesus*

Christ Superstar. Not everything about *Jesus Christ Super-star* or *Godspell* appeals to me, but the fact that they appeared and that people wanted to see and hear them impresses me.

My experience of Jesus may not necessarily fit the pic-ture of Jesus in those contemporary words and those con-temporary melodies. But I have to remember that no two generations ever saw Jesus in exactly the same way. To some degree, every generation sees him as a reflection of itself. We can't help it. And in spite of it the light shines on.

Then I think of how Jesus met his end. How one Friday at high noon the sun hid its face, and darkness fell over the whole land until three in the afternoon. The light of the sun failed, as if to tell me that somehow on his cross Jesus entered into all those dark mysteries that shake my soul—the darkness of isolation, of feeling left out, alienated, and cut off; the darkness of moral anarchy within me, where rage so many conflicting opinions about what I should do that I hardly know my own mind anymore; the darkness of innocent suffering; the darkness of mindless violence loose in the world; and that final darkness, the emptiness of death. Yet on Good Friday there was darkness over the whole land, and until somewhere in life I have felt that kind of darkness, I don't think I'll fully understand the light.

Even the darkness of the grave could not put out the light of God. I suppose the resurrection of Jesus will re-main one of the world's most controversial and mysterious events. Yet I often know and experience the greatest forces in the world not directly but by their effects.

I can't see electricity, but I see the effects of electricity; I see what it does. I can't look straight at the sun, but I feel the sun's warmth and I enjoy it. As I walk in the light of it, I see its effects on nature and in my own life.

No, I can't *see* God, but I can become conscious of his presence through what he does. And after Easter morning the whole world began to see the effect of the resurrection on the lives of some disoriented, despairing people.

The people who walk through the pages of the New Testament—John, Mark, Matthew, Paul, Barnabas, Peter, Mary, Martha, and a host of others—had one thing in common. They differed greatly in personality and temperament, yet they all kept saying, in one way or another, We were in the dark, but we have seen the light.

Not the light of a brighter sun, or the light of better weather, or the light of better government or better schools or more adequate administration of welfare. They spoke of a light that shone in Christ that not even the darkness of dying could extinguish. That light lit up the life they lived.

I've never seen Jesus, if that means seeing someone walking around my city with nailprints in his hands and in his feet. But if "seeing Jesus" means seeing a quality of life take hold of a person and change that person from a self-centered, egotistical bore into a loving, compassionate human being, then, yes, in ways such as this I have seen the Lord.

No dead Christ could transform people in that way. Only a "live" wire can carry current into an electric light bulb. Only a live Christ can bring people to life as he does, lighting up their whole lives.

QUESTIONS FOR REFLECTION AND DISCUSSION

1. In the first ten years of your life, who, outside of your immediate family, contributed most to making you the person you are today? (If you're meeting with a group, the discussion might be started off with this question.)
2. In what way did such people "light up your life"?
3. Where or in what sense do you feel "in the dark" today?
4. Do you think God has ever experienced the darkness you feel?

3. The Flesh and the Word *(1:14–18)*

Many books seem long on process and short on substance, but that's not the feeling John's Gospel gives me. There are no idle words here. To begin with, the writer of the Gospel focuses our attention on one particular time. Of all the billions of moments since time began, he chose to remember one hour, the hour of Jesus' birth.

What makes that moment the center of attention for millions of people up to this day? John wastes no words. He gives it to us in one brief sentence: "The Word became flesh."

Centuries earlier God had given his Word to Moses in stone. Then one day, for better or for worse, the Word of God became flesh. The whole story seems so incredible.

Luke tells us of a dark night suddenly infused with light. There are sights and sounds people had never heard or seen before, and a young mother gets up painfully beside her little boy.

Her husband stands off in the corner thinking how at first it had been just the two of them—a young man and a young woman, wildly in love. And then he remembers the day she first came and told him she was pregnant. How it shook him. And the explanation she gave. Who could swallow a story like that? Suspicion and confusion stretched their love for each other to the breaking point. They had their wedding plans all set, and then "this" happened.

For a while Joseph felt like walking away from the whole thing. He knew one thing for sure: the baby Mary carried was not his. How could he go about believing that "that which is conceived in her is of the Holy Spirit" (Matt. 1:20, RSV)?

He asked Mary again. She said it was true, and he believed her. All kinds of gossip swept through the little Nazarene town, but Joseph stood by this woman he loved. He had stayed by her side through this long, lonely, agonizing night and helped deliver that little boy.

In our world so full of facts and information, achievement, and attainment, people often lose their sense of wonder. Life goes flat with nothing but stale common sense. But in a story like this, everything gets gloriously out of place by everyday standards. A song in the sky, a baby in the barn—"The Word became a human being and lived among us" (TEV).

John's Gospel, along with those of Matthew, Mark, and Luke, is a vignette for us, explaining what people in Galilee and Jerusalem heard God saying through Jesus.

At the age of twelve Jesus proved himself more than a match for the brightest minds of the country, and when he grew up he frequently said the strangest things in the strangest ways. He often seemed disturbingly out of step with the mood of the time.

Once at a wedding Jesus supplied the wine when an embarrassed host found himself running out. He seemed to enjoy the parties and brightened them up. He made friends of some notoriously shady characters. His life had a razor's edge, incisive and cutting. Not an ascetic, not a playboy, he was a real human being.

Once Jesus passed by some caves where lepers lived, and he heard them calling out for mercy and healing. He stopped, reached out his hand, touched the untouchable, and the unclean became whole. No one needed to explain the meaning of the Word to the leper, who knew it in Jesus, and became whole.

Jesus spoke gently with the beaten, the dishonest, the broken. But when he stood face to face with the Pharisees and scribes, they did not fare so well. Jesus said "Hypocrites! You are like tombs covered with whitewash; they look well from outside, but inside they are full of dead men's bones and all kinds of filth" (Matt. 23:27). And that's God's truth. It hurt so much that they determined to silence him forever.

Complex and often bewildering, the Nazarene, in an era of good feelings, said that everything was not right. And then, when people thought the bottom had dropped out of everything, he began to talk about unshakable, immovable foundations. This kind of glorious, incisive Word makes conventional morality look innocuous.

No bland country preacher, this Nazarene carpenter. People either loved him or hated him. But, either way, once they heard him he set them to wondering. Surely if God had stopped to consult us on a plan to save the world, we could have given him some helpful hints on strategy and public relations, how to win friends and influence people. Hints about possibility thinking. Tips on how to be a total woman or a complete man. The Word of God looks a little foolish when you compare it with many of our inspirational ideas and our political insights.

But when John writes, "The Word became a human being," he wants me to understand that, when I see Jesus, I begin to see the way things really are. A good look at him and I begin to get my facts straight. Facts about myself, about human nature, about God, and about this world.

Bernard Baruch once commented to a journalist, "A man has a right to his own opinion, but no man has a right to be wrong in his facts." And Bertrand Russell is quoted as having said of Aristotle, "If a matter is one that can be settled by observation, make the observation yourself. Aristotle could have avoided the mistake of thinking that women have fewer teeth than men by the simple device of asking Mrs. Aristotle to keep her mouth open while he counted. He didn't do so because he thought he knew. Thinking you know when you don't, is a fatal mistake to which we are all prone."

Of course, we're not always so sure we want the truth known. I remember hearing of a western congressman in the midst of a heated campaign who was angered by remarks made about him in editorials of the leading newspaper of one of the communities of his district. One day he burst into the editorial room like a hand grenade and exploded: "You're telling lies about me in your paper, and you know it!"

"Well," said the editor coolly, "you really have no cause for complaint. What in the world would you do if we told the truth about you?"

John believed that in the flesh of Jesus God set the record straight. Yet as I get deeper into John's Gospel I have to admit that the Word God speaks looks foolish when measured by our usual standards. What do you make of a God of supposedly unrestrained power who could not prevent his son from being tortured and killed? How foolish of a God who supposedly never makes a mistake, whose insight never fails, to trust unlearned men with the most profound truth. He didn't choose scientists or philosophers or theologians to teach people the deepest mysteries of life. He chose some young men off the docks and started a youth movement among some marginal people. And in Jesus, God felt the cold winds of our world in his face. He felt the dangers of human temptation and the final, awful loneliness of death.

But behind these words, "The Word became flesh," I hear something I had missed. The Word God speaks is not simply to be understood with my mind; it goes beyond simply learning facts from the Bible. It is what people become. The Word of God is something to *be,* not something to know. God's Word has flesh and bones; it *still* does!

I can learn how to conjugate verbs from a book, but

that kind of learning has little bearing on how I behave and on my values. I learn such personal truths in relationships to other people, in the kind of Word I hear in the flesh of someone I admire. And when I hear it, I begin to value what that person values.

And that is how, says John, the disciples of Jesus heard God's Word—in relationship with someone. As they lived with Jesus, Peter and John and James and the others began to break new ground in their understanding of how to get along in this world and what living a human life means. Word about that began to sink down into their own souls and experience. Sometimes it reminded them of the terrible consequences of their actions, but at other times they felt themselves hearing some glorious music that once split the heavens open. Hearing one bar of that kind of music will do more for a person than years spent studying human depravity.

The disciples discovered a new freedom to live with unanswered questions and unresolved problems. It felt like learning a new language. I remember trying to learn Spanish. When I started, I could pick up a book in Spanish and understand a few words, no more. But I didn't throw the book out and say it didn't make any sense. Instead, I recognized something here and there. But I wasn't sure about the rest. I hoped that some day I'd know the language better, that I'd understand fully. Similarly, while the Word I hear God speaking to me in Christ does not answer all the questions in my mind, it does tell me this: God is for us and with us. He did not come and go as a summer tourist; he is with us yet.

How does God speak today? He once spoke fully in the flesh of Jesus. I believe God is consistent; that is, I believe he still speaks through the Word made flesh. He speaks in the flesh and blood of people. He still makes his Word flesh in people like you and me.

Imagine a young woman lying on her bed in a private room of a veterans' hospital. She's the only woman in an all-male ward, isolated in the midst of people. Does she want cool advice or pious suggestions? Certainly not. She longs for the eyes of someone who will just see her; the ears of someone who will keep quiet and just hear her; the voice of one who will speak in response to her questions.

Some people lose their way because no one has the courage to tell them the truth. If you have children, you realize how difficult that can be. Have you ever tried to talk with them about Christ or about God? Did you feel embarrassed and unsure? Did you know enough? If you love the stars, you certainly have pointed out the North Star or the Big Dipper to your children. If you love flowers you have surely told them something about the blossoms that come and go in the spring and fall. If you love to sail you must have taught them how to sail. If you can show them these things, you can also show them how you pray, how you handle anxieties and hostilities, and how you make sense of the Bible.

What about the people who never show up in church? It's fairly easy for me to talk about Christ with the people in my own congregation, but suppose I had to talk to the people I meet socially or by accident at a lunch counter? How would I do it? By example, of course. We give people the Word by what we do, and I'm all for that. But I realize more deeply than ever that sooner or later they have a right to know what makes us the kind of people we are. Sure, we must share with them the results of our freedom, but should we keep the One who made us free a deep, dark secret? They need the opportunity to know its name, to know what makes you as good as you are at your best. The Word, living in your flesh and blood, can touch their despair with hope, their guilt with mercy, their hatred with love, and open to them the door of new life.

QUESTIONS FOR REFLECTION AND DISCUSSION

1. *What kind of mental picture does the name Jesus arouse on the screen of your imagination?*
2. *In what sense, if any, does the God we know from John's Gospel fail to measure up to what people today expect of God?*
3. *How do you respond to the idea that "the Word of God is something to be"?*
4. *What difference does it make if you expect God to speak through your life?*

4. A Voice in the Wilderness *(1:19–39)*

A voice in the wilderness—surely the last place you'd expect to hear one. Somewhere out in the sand and the wind and the singing silences, the cousin of Jesus got religion, and not just the standard brand either. Out beneath the searing sun and the Syrian stars, eating his organic food, John felt sure he had heard the still, small voice of God.

Then suddenly, like some solitary crag towering above the banks of the Jordan catching the first light of the sun before it reaches the shade of the valleys, there he stood. He blew in like a hot wind off the desert. Like rolling thunder, his voice shook the Jordan Valley.

John attacked entrenched evil in high places and in low. The world around him seemed to have lost touch with sanity. Religion had split up into warring factions: The Pharisees were teaching a morality that nobody could keep; the Sadducees were making the church simply a place to collect and disburse money, and the grim Zealots were determined to root out, in the name of God, anyone they considered uncommitted, disloyal, or subversive. People seemed to have all the little answers without having ever asked the big questions.

In John's view people seemed to have made God's good world a dangerous place in which to live. His concern for pollution went beyond air and water. Like so many people, he had almost given up on organized religion. He did not see it doing the essential kind of thing that its founder, Moses, had done. Mainline religion in John's day no longer upset the Pharaohs of the world. But John did.

He was somewhat like the small boy who, concealing a cap pistol in his pocket before going to church, let the preacher get about halfway through the sermon before whipping out the pistol. At the loud bang that rang out over the congregation everybody seemed to jump about two feet. The father grabbed the boy by the arm and hustled him down the aisle. As he got to one of the back pews, an elderly woman stood and said, "Don't take the boy out. He scared the hell out of more people today than our preacher has in the last ten years."

John affected many people in just that way. He had no regular ordination, no pulpit, no academic gown, and no choir. He was not the Reverend Doctor but just plain John, an honest, angry man taking dead aim at the personal and political dishonesty, greed, and sin that he saw spreading ruin everywhere.

And all kinds of people came to sit by the banks of the Jordan to listen to him—the curious and the hostile as well as the hopeful. Roman soldiers and their Jewish collaborators came, as did the liberal Pharisees, the conservative Sadducees, ragged people out of caves, and the intelligentsia from the university with their endless questions and their empty lives. But then how well do any of us understand the blur of life that goes rushing by? I know people who know more about the internal combustion engines of their cars than they do about the inner workings of their own hearts. How many of us know more about the laws of the physical world around us than we do about the operation of that personal world within? No wonder Carl Jung once wrote, "About one-third of my cases are suffering from no clinical, definable neurosis, but from the senselessness, the emptiness of their lives. They do not understand themselves, and they're unable to live happily with themselves."

When John stopped to catch his breath, people began to ask him questions: John, who are you? Are you the Messiah? Theirs were politically loaded questions, and they waited for an answer. After all, he had a lot of influence, and you never know. . . . Certainly the local politicians wanted to know.

John, if you're not the Messiah, maybe you're Elijah. Malachi had promised that a new Elijah would appear before "the day of the Lord" (Mal. 4:5, RSV) to whip up national and religious enthusiasm. The Messiah would then ride in on its crest. And if you're not Elijah, maybe you're the great prophet Moses promised—someone who'll give us a new Passover and give the Romans a new taste of the Red Sea.

John had one direct, brief answer for each question: *No.* A murmur went through the crowd as John deliberately passed up the greatest opportunities life seemed to offer. And yet each time he said *no,* his identity came more clearly into focus. (I think of how often I discover who I am by that same process of elimination; that is, I discover who I am as I understand who I am not.)

If not the Messiah, nor Elijah, nor the prophet, then who are you, they asked of John.

"I am a voice crying aloud in the wilderness, 'Make the Lord's highway straight,'" he replied.

What a strange answer. This hard, dark, bony desert prophet felt that God wanted to be someone and to do something in history. John invited people to become part of that process and to get ready for it. He wanted people to turn around and put their lives and their society in order, to get ready for the approach of the Lord. People had time to do it. The question was, did they want to?

In this post-Watergate era, I hear people saying, You can't change human nature. That's the way people have always been. That's the way it will go on. And I have to admit, as I watch a growing number of people fall into apathy, that they have a lot of evidence to back up their claim.

A pollster approached one house and rang the bell. An elderly woman opened the door a crack to hear the pollster ask her preference in the coming election. She said, "Vote? I never vote. It just encourages them."

But I've heard others say, Well, everything would be all right if we could just get back to the ethics of our forefathers. I wonder. Did people really live more ethical lives in 1933, or 1900, or 1845? I doubt it. The people who founded this country certainly didn't trust any supposed goodness of the people who lived here. They built an elaborate system of checks and balances into our government precisely because they felt they could not always trust people.

Now what did John mean when he said, "Make the Lord's highway straight"? How does one do that? John had a word for it—*repent.* Unfortunately, the word sounds grimly and depressingly religious. Besides, today we have so few standards left to trespass that *repent* sounds almost obsolete. Society tries less and less often to judge behavior in light of what a person can discover in the Bible. Things we used to call sin now go by the name *realism.* But the effects remain the same. Selfishness, jealousy, envy, greed, and lust all have the same deadly effects on personal life and the life of society in general that they've always had. We can use different terminology, but their effect remains the same.

John believed God had something quite different in mind for life on this planet. He wanted people to get ready to let things happen, to get out of God's way, to begin to get in line with his purpose. And as John talked, people began to feel free to turn in a new direction. Not everybody, of course, but some began to feel released from paralyzing social taboos that had bound them for so long.

When John said "repent," he didn't leave the word hanging vaguely in the air. He committed a preacher's

unforgivable sin: He got specific. That trait cost him his job
and eventually his life. He began to spell out the kind of
changes he meant. The kind of changes in attitude, lifestyle, and behavior.

Government officials who collected taxes asked John
how he would apply his principles to them, and John got
specific. He told them to quit taking bribes and to stop
overcharging people. When soldiers who acted as the law
enforcement officers of the country asked him the same
question, John told them to quit using violence when arresting people, to stop robbing people of their dignity or
their rights, and to stick to the truth when making arrests
(see Luke 3:12–14).

A lot of people took John seriously because they liked
his answers. They went down into the river with him, and
as he poured water over them, they announced to the
world that they would turn and face in the direction of the
God who approached them. They would get ready for
some changes in the way they lived.

Not everyone did that, of course. Most people would
rather suffer than change. Some time ago one of our theological seminaries set up an experiment. A number of students were taken into a small projection room. Then the
instructor went into the room, drew the drapes, closed the
window, and turned the thermostat up to ninety-five de-
grees. Then he gave each student a small toy, left the
room, locked the door, and turned off all the lights. A
strobe light flashed every now and then, and three tape
recorders at full volume blasted music of cacophonous
intensity into the room. After a few minutes, the instructor
sprayed in some cheap perfume followed by sneezing
powder.

The instructors wanted to somehow drive the students
to act responsibly. But they all just sat there sweating,
stinking, sneezing, and feeling miserable. Nobody got up
and pulled the drapes and opened the window. Nobody
turned down the thermostat. They preferred to sit in their

misery than make any small changes in their behavior. A willingness to make those kinds of changes is what John was talking about.

A while ago I received the following letter from a young man in college: "My worst problem is that while I'm settling my hopes and plans with people, I'm afraid that something is missing. Observing my thoughts and actions, I find that I have not given myself to God. I am, in fact, very self-centered and selfish, and I need to find a cure for this dilemma. I'm bogged down with apathy. I wish I could talk to you again. I regret that both times I saw you, I was too afraid to say anything. I feel fully saturated with rational knowledge of God, but also with a great need to know him."

Of course I've talked to other people who aren't looking for God at all. They tell me they find life so full that they don't have time for religious speculation. And at the other extreme, I've talked to people who feel so sure they've found God that they're not looking for him either. Most of the people I know fall somewhere in between, however. They believe God is around, and they're looking for some kind of personal close touch.

One day, as John the Baptist preached, Jesus came to listen. No one knows why he came. An odd sensation came over John and he had trouble remembering his train of thought. He knew Jesus, of course. He knew the keenness of his intellect and the sharpness of his wit. Jesus could strip away the husk of an issue and get right down to the kernel. He was assertive and yet humble, solitary and yet fond of people. John continued to preach, but he felt he had something to say that he had not yet been given. Then Jesus stepped forward and asked John to baptize him. Together they went down into the muddy waters of the Jordan. Suddenly, as John stood hip-deep in the river, something basic happened— something that felt as if heaven itself had split open. And he heard that quiet strong voice he knew so well from the desert: "This is my Son, my Beloved" (Matt. 3:17).

Some years ago an editorial in *Life* magazine contained this arresting sentence: "People have become weary of the words of men. They have lost their confidence in man's ideas, man's programs, man's plans. They are hungry to hear a voice from the other side—a voice of truth, a voice of authority, whose ways will work in the lives of men. . . ."

John heard that voice in one luminous, transforming, sensitizing moment. He knew something now he had never known before. He did not arrive at this new understanding by argument, by some intuitive process of his own mind, or by scientific investigation. Something came to him from beyond, and spoke to something deep inside of him. However difficult it is for modern secular people to accept, that fact remains basic in Christian faith.

People can preach at me about God or Jesus, but only God can make himself known to me. In a sense, people don't come to God at any time they feel like it. They come when God calls them. That makes it a serious thing to trifle with any stirring within that comes from beyond.

So John, his leather clothes dripping water, scrambled back up the bank. His voice cracked with the old authority as he called out to the people, There he is. The one whose approach we've been preparing for. "There is the Lamb of God." That phrase was pregnant to any Jew listening. The lamb symbolized the deliverance; it brought to mind the lamb of Passover killed the night before Moses led the people of God on the greatest freedom march known. It was as though a connection existed between Jesus and God's act to deliver and set his people free.

As John went on preaching, two of his disciples, two of his closest friends, drifted to the edge of the crowd. They saw Jesus begin to walk off down the road, and they followed him. They hadn't gone far before Jesus turned and asked, "What are you looking for?" These are the first words that John records Jesus saying. This is not an accidental peripheral question, but a penetrating one that cuts to the very heart of existence.

The two men following felt the power of the question. They hesitated: "Rabbi, where are you staying?" That is, We don't know what to say. We're not sure what we're looking for. You touched John's life, and he seemed to learn something he could not find out on his own. We want to know what it is. We want to talk to you about it. Where are you staying?

"Come and see," Jesus said. And he didn't mean simply, Come and see where I'm living. He meant, If you're looking for what you say you're looking for, then come with me and you'll see. He didn't give them an explanation; he offered them himself.

After all, explanations do not satisfy the deepest needs I have. I may have questions about death, or, as the title of a recent popular book has it, "life after life," but all the explanations in the world will leave me dead when I die. What Jesus gave these men went beyond ordinary small answers. He did not come to give ideas or information about God. He came to put us in touch with God and with the life of God.

Jesus never confused ideas *about* God with God. There's a great difference. He also knew that you could never trap God between the covers of a holy book. Could the one who once had a hand in getting things started suddenly go home and pull down the shades? No. We hear his voice even yet.

A woman came out of church after a service one Sunday and said to me, "You know, Art, as we worshiped together this morning, I felt tears coming down my face. I caught a glimpse of the glory of God." A few weeks earlier, after church, a man said, "You know, all of a sudden as I sat there, I knew things I had wondered about for years." Glimpses like these will keep a person going for days.

QUESTIONS FOR REFLECTION AND DISCUSSION

1. *How would you describe your feelings toward organized Christianity? Do you think it falls short of what Jesus had in mind? If you could address such Christian leaders as Billy Graham, Pope John Paul II, and Norman Vincent Peale, what would you say to them?*

2. *In what sense can people change, and in what sense does human nature remain the same?*

3. *If you felt God asking you to "repent," how would your daily schedule change? Would anything significant be altered?*

4. *Do you think God can make himself known to you in other ways than your study of the Bible or theology, prayer or the sacraments, or your own personal meditation and inquiry?*

5. You Are: You Shall Be* (1:40–42)

"He never quite knew who he was," said Mrs. Willy Loman of her husband in the tragedy *Death of a Salesman*. When you pass middle age, your tripping becomes less light and more fantastic. More and more people seem to get lost in the shuffle.

Jesus seemed to understand that. At the very start, he said to one of his disciples, " 'You are Simon, son of John. You shall be called Cephas' (that is, Peter, the Rock)."

"You are." "You shall be." The actual and the potential. Jesus saw both with equal clarity, and he saw them together in one person. That means I must be myself now, and I must become all I am meant to be. One part of me seems to define the other.

In John's Gospel, Christ accepts people as he finds them. "You are Simon, son of John." There was no one quite like Simon—intense, vivid, warm. One seldom had to guess what he had on his mind; he let one know. He often took a position on the spur of the moment and then had to look around wildly for some reason to support it. The New Testament tells us more about Simon than any other person, apart from Jesus.

Simon had charisma. Almost everyone has a little of this quality; we couldn't get much done without it. I've seen people who have lots of charisma and little else get a lot of things done.

Simon never did things halfway. He landed sometimes
on the wrong side of an issue and sometimes on the right,
but he never straddled one, unlike the senator who returned home to mend his political fences shortly before an
election. He went around asking his friends, "What's the
main issue around here? I must know what to talk about."

His friends said, "It's the squirrel law. Some people
oppose it; others want the law enforced."

When the senator had talked with several people, he
finally gave a speech. Afterward he invited people to ask
him questions. From way in the back a man asked, "Senator, how do you stand on the squirrel law?"

"Well," said the Senator, "fifty percent of my friends
are for it, and the other fifty percent of my friends are
against it. And I want you people to know that I am for my
friends!"

While Simon never tried to circumvent the hot seat
with that kind of evasion, he did have his weaknesses. He
had the kind of weaknesses that society today often calls
strengths. I remember watching George C. Scott's Acad-
emy Award–winning portrayal of General Patton, who
seemed in the movie to symbolize the same kind of weaknesses. Winning any competition fascinated Patton, who
played to win. As a result he found his whole life filled with
rivals. So did Simon. So do I.

Patton believed in force. His character in the movie
Patton says, "All Americans love the sting of battle. That's
why we've never lost a war." And I remember how Simon
pulled out his sword in the Garden of Gethsemane to cut
down the enemies of Jesus.

Patton had a utilitarian understanding of God. He believed in God, but he also believed that God, for all his
wisdom and understanding, once in awhile needed a little
advice from wise old George Patton. Just before his stun-
ning victory in the relief of Bastogne, Patton called for the
military chaplain. He wanted the chaplain to tell God to
change the weather. The chaplain hesitated but finally

composed this prayer: "Almighty and most merciful Father, we humbly beseech thee out of thy great goodness to restrain these immoderate rains with which we have to contend. Grant us fair weather for battle. Graciously harken to those soldiers who call upon thee, that armed with thy power, we might advance from victory to victory." Patton found nothing offensive in that prayer.

Simon once had a great revelation. He said he had discovered God's Messiah in Jesus. Jesus said to him, Simon, you didn't think that up on your own. God opened your eyes to it. And Jesus went on to explain what being God's Messiah would mean in this kind of world, how he was heading for a cross. At that point Simon took him aside to give him a little wise counsel: Lord, we'll never let that happen. And you can't let it happen. It just *won't* happen. Jesus shook him off by saying, Get behind me, you devil. You don't understand anything at all (see Matt. 16:21–23).

I'm beginning to see who Simon actually is. He's a person so like myself, who so easily mistakes weakness for strength, is fascinated by winning every competition, forcing every issue, giving God some advice to achieve personal ends. That's who *I* am.

But Jesus sees more—more in Simon and more in me. He also sees who you are and who you shall be. What potential Jesus saw in Simon! He saw a person who lived with his eyes open, who looked for more in life than he had yet seen. Where could he find it? By what criteria would he define it? Once he'd seen it, what would he do? How could he let loose the potential he felt built into him? So many people die with their music still in them.

I rowed on the crew team as an undergraduate at the University of California. Later, while attending Princeton Theological Seminary, I coached the lightweight crews at Princeton University. I still remember starting out as a freshman, sitting in the freshman locker room upstairs in the boathouse listening to Russ Nagler, the freshman coach, explain how to go about rowing a boat. I did my best to translate what he said into how I handled an oar, but I couldn't put it together very well.

Then one day I saw a fellow rowing in the varsity boat who incarnated the principles Nagler spoke of. I said to myself, I'll use him as a model. I'm going to be like him. That decision marked a turning point in my life as an athlete. I learned later that sociologists call it finding a role model. This distinction is not new, but it is crucial. A small child may obey his parents' commands, at least to the extent that he understands. But that's different from admiring your father and discovering you have the capacity to be like him.

Something like that happens to most of us at one time or another. To some it happens more dramatically than to others, yet we all come to those kinds of turning points in our lives. Consciously or unconsciously, we pick someone who embodies what we're looking for, and we say to ourselves, I'm going to be like him or her.

When Andrew, Simon's brother, and some of his friends first ran into Jesus, something about him made Andrew ask, "Where are you staying?"

Jesus answered, "Come and see." So they went, and they stayed all day. Andrew began to sense in Jesus something he thought his brother Simon had looked for for years, so he ran to tell him: Simon, I think I've found it. For a minute I caught a glimpse of what we've been looking for (see 1:44).

Simon dropped his nets and ran to meet this solidly built carpenter with the rough, calloused hands and the clear eyes of a man used to taking the measure of things. This was no ordinary carpenter. Simon knew his brother had made no mistake. This stranger from Galilee marked a turning point in Simon's life.

I didn't meet Jesus the way Simon did or the way Paul did, though some people may. I believe mystical occurrences such as Paul had on the road to Damascus remain very real. Some people today meet Jesus the way Francis

of Assisi did. He picked up the New Testament and read
Matthew's Gospel. Behind and beneath the words he read
he heard someone saying to him, Francis, take nothing for
your journey. Take no gold, no silver, no copper in your
belt, no staff, not two tunics or pairs of sandals. And he did
it.

I met Jesus in the flesh of people who knew him
and lived close to him. I remember meeting him in the
life of one of San Francisco's leading attorneys, who,
when he was in his sixties, used to take time every Sunday evening to sit down with high school young people.
I met Christ again in college in the life of an imagina-
tive preacher, then again in the life of a doctor who en-
couraged me and believed in me when I started out as
a young minister, trying to get my feet on the ground.
I met him later in the life of a wholesale produce man
in Fresno, California. And again and again in countless
people since, the spirit of Jesus Christ confronts me. No
one person contains the whole of Christ. None of us
perfectly reflects his image. Yet he meets me in the
lives of his people.

So Simon fell in step with Jesus. And the more he
listened to him and lived with him, the more he became like him. That's how the Christian movement
began—people getting close to Jesus. Along the way
Simon had lapses and flagged more than once. But he
saw in Jesus the kind of person he always felt he
wanted to be. I find that happening in my life, too.
Christ, in a variety of ways, helps me see the kind of
person I am. That's terribly important. But the more I
see of him, the more I discover the kind of person I
shall become. That's far more important still. Jesus saw
in Simon a man with an imperfect background but a
bright future. And I believe that's what he sees in you
and me. "You are: you shall be."

QUESTIONS FOR REFLECTION AND DISCUSSION

1. The media manager of a major political candidate told him, "You'll never get elected if you insist on substituting substance for style." How would you describe the style of life you'd like to live? What relation should such a lifestyle have to the substance of your life?

2. Do you find anything offensive in the prayer offered by the chaplain of General Patton's forces before the battle of Bastogne?

3. What role models for life did you have as a young person? What role models do you have now?

4. Do you think God believes in your future? What evidence do you have for or against that idea?

6. The Life of the Party
(2:1–11)

It's a funny thing about parties. You can never tell how they'll turn out. Sometimes my conscience drives me to arrange a get-together for a number of people to whom I owe invitations. I find myself muttering, "I'd give an arm and a leg to get this thing over with." But then during dinner, or maybe afterward, something happens that ignites the evening and everyone, including me, has a roaring good time.

At other times, when I've invited an "all-star cast" and have expected one of the galas of the season, the party dies on its feet. Desperately I look across the room for the sourest looking person I can find and ask, "How's that big project of yours coming?" If he doesn't have a big project, nine times out of ten he'll think of one. Not tonight. When the last guest leaves 45 minutes later I feel like going under for the third time.

Jesus, a born mixer, loved parties. He knew how to have a good time. So far as I can discover, he never turned down an invitation, nor did he ever seem out of place. He had a yen for people—the rich and the powerful, the poor and the oppressed, Roman soldiers, intellectual Pharisees, corrupt government officials, lepers, harlots, children.

John, who began his Gospel with the mind-boggling statement "The Word became flesh; he came to dwell among us," now wants us to see and feel how the human presence of God looked and acted. No more philosophical ideas.

He starts with the story of Jesus at a party. "On the third day there was a wedding at Cana-in-Galilee. The mother of Jesus was there, and Jesus and his disciples were guests also." Some of the followers of John the Baptist openly criticized Jesus for not simplifying his life the way John had done. You'd never catch John the Baptist at a noisy wedding reception. If he'd gone, he probably would have ruined the party. This stern, unyielding prophet of reform spent all his energy denouncing irresponsibility. In a world full of hungry and poor people, the followers of John saw Jesus as an irresponsible wine bibber and glutton.

It's not that Jesus condoned irresponsibility or exploitation. He simply accepted people where he found them. And when people felt that kind of acceptance, instead of the usual rejection, they found their lives beginning to change.

That's why this story of Jesus begins with a party, and with something Jesus did rather than said. It's characteristic of the Bible to have events precede theology. Lights, action, camera—that's the way the Bible reads.

Jesus doesn't seem at all out of place at the party. In fact, if he had not been there, it would have died on its feet. If we're going to get inside John's Gospel, we have to accept the story of what happened at the party as it stands without trying to spiritualize it away. Like any good reporter, the writer of the Gospel gives us the facts, which is what modern people want. We don't want to be fooled, particularly in matters of religion. How can I know the truth unless I keep my eyes wide open to the facts and honestly try to come to terms with them.

When did the party happen? Well, the story starts out, "On the third day." In other words, two days after Jesus finally got together the men he wanted to make disciples out of.

Where did it happen? "At Cana-in-Galilee." Now that's

a precise location I can find on a map today. In fact, I can get on a plane in Los Angeles one day, get off in Tel Aviv the next day, and have dinner at Cana-in-Galilee the following day.

To whom did it happen? "The mother of Jesus was there." She didn't stand around like a plaster saint, either. She acted like a lot of mothers do when they want a grown son to do something—she tried to take charge. "Jesus and his disciples were guests also." That means Mary had received the invitation. Jesus and the twelve men with him came as an afterthought. When the bridegroom heard that they had arrived in town, he probably said to Mary, Well, bring them along. So we have the mother of Jesus, Jesus and his disciples, and the steward, who acted as caterer, master of ceremonies, and coordinator of the whole event.

And what happened? "The wine gave out." We don't know why. Did the unexpected arrival of Jesus and twelve extra men put a strain on the supply? After all, Jesus and his disciples had the reputation of being wine bibbers already. Or had the host simply misjudged the capacity of his guests? The story doesn't explain, it just says that the mother of Jesus said to him, "They have no wine left." Who knows what she thought he could do about it.

Jesus' answer didn't give her much encouragement. "Your concern mother, is not mine." What a great way to say, Don't try to tell me what to do. It isn't any of our business. So they ran out of drinks. Too bad. But it's up to them. The mother of Jesus needed to know that he had not come into the world simply to fill empty wine glasses.

The mother of Jesus knew her son, however, and she felt sure he'd do something. So she said to the servants, "Do whatever he tells you." And she was right. Soon Jesus spotted the empty stone wine jars. He asked the servants to fill them with water. And then he said, "Draw some off." They did and took it to the steward, who tasted it and called the bridegroom over. "Everyone serves the best wine first," he said, "and waits until the guests have drunk freely before serving the poorer sort; but you have kept the best until now." What a sense of humor Jesus had. He knew how to laugh and how to make other people laugh.

But it was a miracle, wasn't it? I believe it was, though you don't have to. No one will go to hell because he doesn't believe that Jesus turned water into wine—not grape juice, wine. Yet if the essence of God took on human flesh, then it seems to me anything wonderful could happen. If God has visited us in Christ, then the rest is easy.

In a recent book, *A Rumor of Angels*, sociologist Peter Berger notes that modern people understand the degree to which the views of people in other eras were colored by the culture of their day. But, he points out, it never seems to occur to us that the assumptions of the culture we live in equally condition or warp our attitudes. For instance, our culture conditions us to assume a miracle story must be false. Why? Because everyone knows miracles don't happen. We assume that's a scientific point of view.

Of course it isn't. Science tells me, through what I can see and touch and measure, what usually happens. It does not and it cannot rule out the possibility that the author of the system might occasionally introduce an additional cause into the natural process and achieve an effect quite different from the usual. The additional cause, in a genuine miracle, is simply the will of God to have it happen.

I don't want to overdogmatize how the miracle at Cana happened or what the details were. But I remember that in the end, when people wanted to get rid of Jesus, it was not because they failed to notice what he did. If Jesus had simply stuck to teaching, the people would hardly have decided to kill him. Those hardheaded politicians knew the impotence of ideals and moral appeals. Jesus' teaching didn't scare them, but his actions did. They crucified him not so much for what he said as for what he did.

That's why my question about the miracles of Jesus has never been whether they *happened*. My question remains, *why* did they happen? What's the point?

At first glance, this turning of water into wine seems to have no socially redeeming value. At the time it happened, thousands of people went to bed hungry in Israel. Yet there's Jesus enjoying himself at a party and providing the drinks. He doesn't act like so many grim do-gooders pressing for social justice. How many of them would have thought to help an embarrassed middle-class bridegroom out of a jam?

Such a view oversimplifies the challenge we all face of integrating and ordering priorities. Like Jesus, we all have to wrestle with the problem of how to avoid becoming a gluttonous pig on the one hand or an abstemious prig on the other.

Still, what has any of this water-to-wine business to do with you and me? Why tell us this story? Because I need to know how God gets things done in this world, and in my life. How did Jesus save this party? He did it with the help of some very human hands. He had to have the cooperation of the servants. If they had not filled the stone jars with water, nothing would have happened. Jesus always worked that way. When he had five thousand people to feed, what did he do? He asked his disciples for help. And he couldn't have done it at all if he hadn't found that nameless boy with a little bit of lunch in his pocket. Jesus once healed a paralytic. Why? Because four determined friends tore open the roof and let the fellow down into the room where Jesus sat. Jesus never could have done anything if everyone he ran into felt like the small boy who, when asked which story in the Bible he liked best, replied, "That one about the multitude—you know, the multitude that loafs and fishes."

The miracles of God wait for your cooperation and mine. Yes, God sends the rain and the sunshine, but the farmer has to do his part. Faith is an activity; it is something I do. Faith is not merely agreeing with religious ideas. In his Gospel, John never uses the noun *faith* at all. Rather, he uses the verb *to believe*—a verb describing activity. Belief means doing something.

Such believing has a person as its object. John never asks, *What* do you believe? He always asks, In *whom* do you believe? I'm beginning to understand my faith as a process of relating to, and cooperating with, the God who comes to meet me in Jesus Christ.

As we've seen, the miracles of God come at the hands of some very human people. Yet a fine line exists between religious superstitions and miracles. My wife, Millie, worked for a time in oncology research at the University of Southern California Medical Center in Los Angeles. A young woman came in for treatment and made remarkable progress through chemotherapy. She returned to an active, normal life with an excellent prognosis.

Suddenly she decided not to take her medicine any longer. She had gone to a "miracle service" and said she came out feeling completely healed. She felt God would take care of everything from then on. She did get along fine for several weeks. Then one day when she was out water-skiing, she began to hemorrhage and came back to the hospital simply to die.

I believe God heals and I believe all healing comes from God, but my faith does not work the way that young woman tried to make hers work. I believe I cooperate with God when I receive at some very human hands the best that medical science can prescribe. The fact that God uses human intelligence and human hands takes nothing away from the miracle of healing itself.

Christ asks us to do all we can, just as he asked the servants at the party to fill the empty jars with water. Then we stand back and allow God to do what none of us can do. Those servants filled the jars; then they drew some off. But what a surprise! What a contrast between the pale, tasteless water that went in and what they drew out.

Of course, Jesus did not come primarily to turn water into wine at weddings, but he did come to let loose the kind of power that can save people from disaster. If he can really still do that, what great good news for father or mother or child. All his life Jesus ran into people from whom the wine of life had run out—for the leper, it was the wine of hope; for the man who beat his breast and said, "God be merciful to me a sinner," it was the wine of good conscience; for Mary and Martha at the death of their brother, it was the wine of comfort.

Even today I run into people who feel as if "they have no wine left." As young people, they reached out with anticipation, but when they had their hands on whatever they had so eagerly reached for, they didn't feel satisfied. Fed up at forty, fagged out at fifty. One man looked his doctor right in the eye and said, "Doctor, I've tried everything, but I've ended up with nothing. I have a nice house. I have a swimming pool. I have two cars—both Cadillacs. I've done everything I ever wanted to do. I have everything a person could wish for, except the ability to wish for anything. Doctor, I've come to the point where I just don't give a damn anymore."

That's hardly surprising, really. The man had followed a perfect formula for boredom. Anybody can achieve it simply by narrowing down his or her interests and thinking that the satisfaction of life can be found in satisfaction of the physical senses. That's why life sometimes sours for people, and turns, before they drink the last drops, to acid.

But where Jesus found people willing to cooperate with him, he filled their lives with gladness. He left a trail of joy behind him. Jesus ran into a grasping internal revenue agent named Levi and set him to work writing the Gospel of Matthew. He found a woman out of her mind with guilt and anxiety and made her the first herald of his resurrection. He found a rigid intellectual, fiercely committed to defend the orthodoxy of his faith, and turned him into the church's foremost progressive apostle.

"This deed at Cana-in-Galilee is the first of the signs by which Jesus revealed his glory and led his disciples to believe in him."

QUESTIONS FOR REFLECTION AND DISCUSSION

1. In a world full of hungry and poverty-stricken people, why do you think Jesus took the time to go to a fancy wedding party?
2. After you reached twenty-one, did you ever have a parent try to get you to do something? How did you react, and why?
3. In what sense, if any, do you think a set of facts exists other than the facts of science or history?
4. Do you think that "the miracles of God wait for your cooperation and mine"? Do you have any evidence from your own experience for thinking this?

7. Blowing in the Wind

(3:1–21)

Charles Colson, a member of President Richard Nixon's administration, wrote a book called *Born Again* about his conversion and changed life after the Watergate affair. Later, Billy Graham, who had earlier published a book titled *Angels,* is reputed to have phoned Colson and asked, "Charles, would you mind if I called my next book *How to Be Born Again*"?

"Not at all," Colson is said to have replied. "I'm thinking of calling my next book *How to Become an Angel.*"

That Colson's book *Born Again* sold over two million copies and Graham's *How to Be Born Again* had a very large first press run tells me that something is blowing in the wind. According to recent polls, one-third of all Americans say they have had a "born-again" experience.

I've discovered that such talk usually takes place on two levels. A lot of it stays right on the surface. People talk about their experiences with the same detachment with which they talk about the next primary election, or a new tax policy, or the movie *Oh God!* Though often very stimulating talk, it does not go very deep.

People often tried to get Jesus into such discussions. The Pharisees wanted to argue about what they could or couldn't do on the Sabbath. The Sadducees wanted to argue about life after life. They didn't believe in it, but they wanted to argue with Jesus.

Sometimes when we're talking about God the talk takes a plunge beneath the surface, either suddenly or gradually. When it does, I find I'm beyond exchanging ideas—I'm involved personally. I no longer talk about God; he is an active participant in the conversation. This kind of talk can change a person's whole life, and often it does.

In John's Gospel we see that Jesus seldom lets talk about God remain on the surface, though once he plunges me beneath it, I find no clear, logical progression. I get no quick, snappy answers. Nor do I find any clear conclusion to the conversation; it seems to go on and on.

Sometimes late at night questions arise from beneath the superficial things of life and take me by the throat. During the day I get along pretty well. I can write letters, talk, do what I think needs doing. But then night comes, and with it other questions, deeper questions.

John writes, "There was one of the Pharisees named Nicodemus, a member of the Jewish Council, who came to Jesus by night." Nicodemus, one of the most popular preachers in the capital city, had little time for the Sadducees and their dependence on the military-industrial complex of Rome. He had no patience for the Essenes, who would rather drop out and head for the desert to form a communal counterculture. And he certainly had no stomach for the Zealots, who plotted terrorist acts to blow up whatever authority they could.

No, as a Pharisee, Nicodemus wanted to preserve the finest values his country and people had produced. Yet, with the coming of Jesus, he, too, sensed something blowing in the wind. "Rabbi," he said. "We know that you are a teacher sent by God." (A brilliant opening for some discussion, a little theology perhaps, or a debate.) But Jesus did not beat around the bush.

Quite a difference exists between beating the bushes and beating around the bush. Both phrases come from medieval England. When an Englishman went on a wild boar hunt, he took people with him to beat the bushes and drive out the wild animal. But a wild boar can rip you to ribbons, and people knew it. So very often, instead of going into the bush to beat it, they simply "beat around the bush."

That's the way Nicodemus started. Coming to the point can be risky, though in our post-Watergate era people no longer have a stomach for evasiveness. Neither did Jesus. He would not beat around the bush. He wasted no time on surface chatter about religion. "In truth, in very truth I tell you, unless a man has been born over again he cannot see the kingdom of God." From there on Nicodemus lost the initiative. He wanted a little surface talk, an exchange of information. He had expected nothing like this. He found himself stammering some nonsense about trying to get back into his mother's womb, like the comic-strip character Charlie Brown, who asked Lucy, "How do you expect me to learn new math with an old math brain?" He may have regretted he'd come. Clearly he couldn't handle Jesus' analogy.

Jesus had suddenly plunged him beneath the surface of life, as if to say, My friend, neither of us has much time left. You know a lot of things and you have a lot of questions, but even if you had the answers to those questions, would it really help you? Before we try to solve the problems of the world, let's come to grips with *your* problems. Some very primitive things play decisive roles in your life: your stomach needs food; your conscience needs peace; your whole being cries out for life, while you move irresistably toward death. You don't need information. You need a new beginning so basic that the only effective analogy I can find is the analogy of birth. Nicodemus, I'm talking about an inner freshening. Flesh can give birth only to flesh; it's the Spirit that gives birth to spirit.

My spiritual life begins when something comes over me—something I cannot see; something I cannot predict; something I cannot analyze; something I cannot explain, at least not at the time. Something like the wind. Mysterious? Yes. Puzzling? Not necessarily. It becomes a puzzle only when people try to reduce spiritual birth and life to some arbitrary cut-and-dried formula.

Nicodemus said, "But how is it possible?"

And Jesus answered, What? You, the preacher of Israel, and you don't understand this? If *you* don't understand it, Nicodemus, how can anybody else? We don't hear anything more from Nicodemus that night.

I have an idea that a lot of people today have as much trouble with the phrase *born again* as Nicodemus did. After all, Jesus used it only once. He only asked it of one person. He didn't try it with the woman at the well, or the man blind from birth, or the rich young ruler, or anyone else in the New Testament.

But a lot of people use it today. It's just that many who do don't use it in a way that clarifies what Jesus meant. They simply make it harder for us to understand. Even Jesus bewildered Nicodemus.

I can do several things with the phrase *born again*. I can pretend it doesn't exist. I can leave it for "super-Christians" to talk about over religious television. Or I can stick with it until the meaning begins to break in upon my mind and upon my life. And, of course, that's what I choose to do. I can't give this text up; I can't ignore it, leaving it to others to interpret in any way they see fit. With two words, Jesus plunges me beneath the surface and asks me to grapple with the essence of the Christian experience.

The whole analogy calls for a radical reorientation in our lives. Suppose for a minute that people couldn't change. Suppose we could freeze the status quo. What would a static world feel like? If changes in human nature cannot happen, then I am stuck with myself as I am. My mediocre mind could not develop; the deep divisions inside of me, tearing me apart, would continue deep divisions forever, unhealed, unrelieved, unresolved. I could never escape my frustrations. If change in human nature is not possible, we're stuck with monstrous evils on our hands. What better description of hell could anyone have?

I remember hearing, as a boy, You're never too old to learn. I didn't think about it much then, but now that I'm older, often that thought comes back. And when it does, I wonder if people do not reach a time in life when the mind closes, and nothing much passes through it. Nothing much new, that is. I wonder whether you *can* ever teach an old dog new tricks. Age has its own tricks to play on us.

But from within John's Gospel, Jesus helps me see that if I repudiate the possibility of a radical change in the quality of my life, I repudiate God himself! I then say that the situation in my life, the present situation in the world, with all its evils, represents the mind of God. If things can't or shouldn't change, then the present situation is the best God can do. Who wants a god like that? What kind of ethics could we possibly have?

Jesus insists that hope for the present and the future rests in the possibility of a dynamic reorientation in the lives of individuals and their communities. To Jesus, the phrase *born again* means born from above. He talks about an experience over which I have no more control than I did my physical birth. He means something God does.

Can a person change habits and characteristics formed over a period of ten or twenty or thirty years? Yes, Jesus insists. He also insists you can't ask which comes first, faith or new birth. They go together, both as an act and as a process.

Jesus spoke out of his own experience. After all, he changed as he lived through adolescence into maturity. Luke described him like this: "He advanced in wisdom and in favor with God and men" (Luke 2:52). That means God acted in the humanity of Jesus to get our humanity moving in a new direction—a direction we can participate in and be part of. And that's what's blowing in the wind.

Jesus went on to say, "The wind blows where it wills; you hear the sound of it, but you do not know where it comes from, or where it is going. So with everyone who is born from spirit." I've seen desert sands suddenly whipped by this powerful, invisible force. I've seen trees bend before it. I've watched a calm ocean lashed into whitecaps by the same mysterious power. I cannot capture the wind, unlike fire or water—"Who has gathered the wind in his fists?" (Prov. 30:4, RSV). But I can see the effects of it. About the only thing we can predict of the wind, I suppose, is its direction.

Jesus said the Spirit of God operates like that. Visibly, intangibly, in a way we cannot capture with our minds. We don't know his origin, we don't know his destination; but we can see the effects of his presence and the direction in which he moves. Paul wrote, "The harvest of the Spirit is love joy, peace, patience, kindness, goodness, fidelity, gentleness, and self-control" (Gal. 5:22). When I see such things loose in human life, I know I stand in the presence of the living God just as surely as when I hear the rustling of the wind through the trees in the park. The birth of God's Spirit in a person's life begins to produce those fruits Paul speaks of.

C. S. Lewis once compared this qualitative kind of change to the development of an egg. New life must hatch out of an egg, or the egg will begin to decay and stink. In the same way, I cannot attempt to preserve my christian heritage or faith as it was or is. It will begin to stink unless a really different kind of life emerges from it.

From the very beginning, Jesus ran into trouble with some of the finest people he knew. He lived out of this deeper dimension of life—a life wide open to the Spirit of God. And that produced in him an inner dynamic that external circumstances could not touch, let alone shatter. Because of this, he went through death and hell into the presence of our Father.

That is what continues to blow in the wind. Listen, Nicodemus, Jesus said. You can hear what I'm saying about blowing in the wind. You hear the wind and see what it does. What God has produced in my life he can begin to produce in yours. It will happen when the Spirit of God blows through you and clears out the dust of old prejudices and lifeless dogma. You can't make the wind blow. It's already blowing. You don't have to chase after life as though you could catch it in your hands. All you need to do is open yourself to it. You can't bring on birth from above any more than you could bring on your physical birth. But God can and will. Your spiritual birth may have very little to do with chills running up and down your spine. It won't result in your becoming a self-realized or self-actualized person. In fact, you will suddenly lose interest in your own salvation. That's a preoccupation you need saving from. Suddenly you will find yourself making common cause with people who hurt, people you have overlooked. And no one's too old to learn that.

Here beneath the surface, regardless of what reservations I may have had or how obtuse and narrow I find a lot of Christian thought, the question suddenly becomes, Am I willing to take a chance and bet my life that Jesus is right? He never asks me to affirm an intellectual certainty I do not have, but he continually confronts me with the fact that, though I may put off making up my mind, I cannot put off making up my life. Whether I like it or not, I will live either as though God is real or as though he is simply an ancient symbolic figure.

Jesus described the result of allowing the wind of God to blow through my life as "eternal life." He didn't say everlasting life. He didn't mean life that simply goes on and on and on. (I remember as a child how that worried me. What would I do forever?) You can feel the difference between *everlasting* and *eternal;* it's a qualitative difference. Everlasting music simply goes on and on, until it seems it will drive you out of your mind. Eternal music has something of the essence of life to it. Such music moves one deeply. And when Jesus spoke of eternal life, he meant an essential quality of life that continues to expand in its liveliness in every conceivable human dimension in and beyond time.

"The wind blows where it wills; you hear the sound of it, but you do not know where it comes from, or where it is going. So with everyone who is born from spirit."

QUESTIONS FOR REFLECTION AND DISCUSSION

1. *Have you ever heard a sermon that explained the Gospel of Jesus Christ in a way that ran counter to some of your most valued traditions? How did you feel? What did you do?*

2. *A growing number of people say they have had a "born-again" experience. Why do you think Jesus used this phrase only once, and then in a private conversation rather than in a sermon to the general public?*

3. *Do you think you will become irreversibly set in your ways as you grow older? What new ideas have you embraced in the last year? In the last ten years?*

4. *Do you see any difference between* eternal life *and* everlasting life? *If so, what does the difference mean for you?*

8. Beneath the Surface
(4:1–30)

Sinclair Lewis once told in an interview of a man caught up in an affair with a woman who, as they lay in bed one afternoon, said to him, "You know, on the surface we seem quite different, but deep down we're basically the same. We're both desperately unhappy about something and we don't know what it is." A person can skip along on the surface from partner to partner, hoping to find that something, but no one can forever avoid sinking.

Just suppose that something lies beneath the surface, as I believe it does. John's Gospel, one of the oldest books around, has helped me penetrate the depths. John shows us Jesus sitting at high noon beneath a blazing sun by Jacob's old well. He looks tired and hot and thirsty. Hunger can be placated for a while, but not thirst. The thirstier we get, the more we want to drink. So I watch Jesus and notice he has no way of getting water from the well. Then, hearing footsteps, he stirs. He looks up, looks away, and then looks up again at the woman standing beside him. She's the kind of woman who would make any man look twice. She knows it and doesn't care.

Maybe you've seen her. Nowadays she lives in a fancy condominium, manages to look ten years younger than her age, enjoys a swinging social life, and holds down a prestigious and well-paying job. If you look closely, however, you can see lines of cynicism in her face, and a haunting sadness around her eyes. She no longer expects anything different or better from life.

This beautiful woman knows that everything comes with a price tag. As Hoover Rupert once noted, after every meal somebody has to wash the dishes. That's the price of eating. If you live by yourself, you may let dishes pile up in the sink, but sooner or later somebody has to wash them or you'll run out. Even in a restaurant the price of a meal extends beyond its prepar to the washing of those dirty dishes. We'd rather not think about it, particularly in reference to our own behavior, but eventually, inevitably, *somebody* has to wash up. And the dirty dishes in the life of this beautiful woman by the well have begun to accumulate.

When Jesus saw her, he spoke right up, though a lot of men would have had trouble doing that. They feel terribly threatened in the presence of an attractive woman. When they *do* speak, their palms sweat and their tongue feels like marble. They feel silly and sound stupid because they're trying to make an impression, unlike this Galilean who seemed at ease sitting besides Jacob's well. The two of them were so different: he was a man, she a woman; he was a Jew, she a Palestinian. In spite of that, he spoke as if they both had the same insides.

I remember a young boy who came home from a camping trip, threw his pack in the middle of the living room floor, kicked off his muddy shoes, and left them where they fell. His mother had cleaned house all day. At the angry sound of his name on her lips, he knew he had made a big mistake. Soon his father joined in. All evening the boy couldn't seem to do anything right, so he took refuge in his room. Before long, however, his father came in to chide him for the terrible, thoughtless thing he'd done. The boy sat slumped in his chair with big tears welling at the corners of his eyes and screamed, "Nobody understands me! I'm lonely."

That outburst stopped the father in mid-sentence. He

sat down on the bed and, after a few minutes, said, "Son, thank you for saying that. I'm sorry we have the kind of relationship where you never felt free to say it before. I want to tell you something you ought to know. Your mother and father are very lonely people. Did you know that? Did you know that everybody else on this block is lonely too?"

We all have the same insides, though we may look different and may have different religious and political prejudices. But the father found that, as he shared his own loneliness with his son, he opened up new possibilities for fulfillment for both of them.

No wonder Jesus spoke to the woman first. He didn't begin by saying, I don't think I've seen you in church lately, but rather by asking her a favor. He needed something badly and put himself at her mercy by saying, "I'm thirsty, could you give me a drink?"

Nothing puts people at ease as quickly as asking them for help, which Jesus often did. Once he asked for a boat and rowed out into the lake to teach the people on shore. How excited he made a little boy by asking for his lunch to feed a great crowd; how quickly Zacchaeus scrambled down that tree when Jesus asked if he could come home for lunch with him. At the last, Jesus asked a friend to loan him his donkey to ride into Jerusalem.

I grew up thinking about how Jesus helped other people. I knew he cheered them up, forgave their sins, healed their diseases, and shook up their consciences; but I had forgotten, if I ever knew, how many times he asked people for a favor. He asked this woman for a drink; he asked Matthew, Peter, and John, to give up their business and follow him. Later on he asked them to "feed my sheep" (21:17), and "sit here while I pray" (Mark 14:32). Jesus had some very real human needs that only other people could satisfy.

Those needs of Jesus prompt me to think about what we call the "body of Christ," the church. For years I looked to the church for what God would do for me—for my spirit, for my soul. Whenever I looked for a church, I looked for one that offered *me* something, that would steady me, teach me, feed me, encourage me, and give me friendship. I believe that the church exists to serve people's bodies and souls. Through it we feed hungry people and help them in a hundred other ways.

Yet now I hear Jesus asking someone to do something for his body; I hear him asking this woman for a drink. Behind those words I hear God's voice urging me, Art, the body of Christ still needs the kind of things that only people like you can give it. Give that tired, thirsty body your support. Give it your interest, your time, your energy, and your money. Christ needs you. He needs what you can do for his body.

I realize now that a church never really helps me by simply doing things for me. I get help from a church that brings me to the point of doing something for the body of Christ, and through it for the lives of other people.

Jesus asked the woman for a drink and tried to put her at ease, but I have a feeling she suspected something right from the start. She came at high noon purposely to avoid meeting people. She questioned how he could ask her for a drink. An Israeli man putting himself at the mercy of a Palestinian woman? As usual, Jesus didn't give a straight answer. People had an awful time with that trait in Jesus. They'd ask him a straight question and he wouldn't give them a straight answer. But he did it for a very good reason. He wanted to help people get beneath the surface of their lives, to draw them out and help them think. So instead of explaining to her that he didn't care about the artificial differences between Jews and Palestinians, he said, If only you knew . . . who it is that is asking you for a drink, you would have asked him and he would have given you living water. His words were confusing, yet she knew in a flash that he didn't mean literal water. She wasn't sure that he meant any kind of water. If he wanted from her what most men wanted when they saw her body, he certainly had a different line.

So she said, "You have no bucket and this well is deep. How can you give me 'living water?' " Jesus' puzzling statement had begun to bring her beneath the surface of life. She started to think beyond the way she usually did. Living water? What does that mean?

In 1977 California suffered a drought, but with 1978 the rains came and the Bureau of Water Conservation became the Bureau of Flood Control. Water means different things to different people in different circumstances. We need water to drink, water to irrigate farms, and water for baths and showers. Reading or hearing the word *water* can bring to mind a refreshing swim in a pool on a warm summer day or the memory of being caught in a riptide. Does the word *water* mean the same thing to one sailing a boat across a sunny harbor as it does to someone who has just escaped a spring flood?

In the Bible the word *water* appears in various contexts. Many of the writers of the Bible saw water as a threat to their lives: They tell of a flood covering the whole earth; they describe the Red Sea swallowing the armies of Pharaoh; Jesus says, "The rain came down, the floods rose, and the wind blew, and beat upon that house; down it fell with a great crash" (Matt. 7:27).

The Bible also speaks of water as life. Yes, the flood covered the earth, but that same water floated Noah's ark. Yes, the water destroyed Pharaoh's army, but that same water saved the people of Israel for the land of promise.

Finally this woman at the well sensed that the man beside her wanted not her body but her soul, and that was even worse! It dawned on her that they had talked of water in two different ways. As Theodore Parker Ferris observed, she meant something from life and he meant something from God. If a man asks me how to get to San Francisco, I take out my map and show him. But if a young person whom I know and love asks me the way to San

Francisco, I say, "If you want to get to San Francisco, do the best job you can where you are now." In the first instance I mean a way of travel, while in the second I mean a way of life.

Jesus always uses words to get me beneath the surface of life. He wants to get my attention off the immediate necessities and onto the ultimate satisfactions. Of *course*, I need water for my body; yes, I need food; certainly, I need money to pay my bills. Jesus, never underestimating any of that, heals the sick and feeds the hungry. But he also knows that I might settle for having my basic needs cared for, a mortgage on its way to being paid off, a car, and other things that make life easier, and neglect the ultimate things—the inner things, those things that pull life together and bring happiness and direction and make a person useful.

Gradually it dawned on this woman how thirsty she had grown for what no water and no money and no bread and no sex could ever satisfy. God knows how desperately she had tried to get more out of this world than there is in it. She felt thirsty for a cleaner, better, fuller way of living, but she and God had fallen out a long time before. She wasn't sure she wanted anything to do with him, nor was she quite sure he wanted anything to do with her. "Sir, give me that water."

What a shock it was to hear Jesus say, "Go home. Call your husband." The words shot through her like fire, as her domestic disorder was abruptly laid bare. Those words took her back many long years to girlhood, to that first bright-eyed boy out in the vineyards of Gerizen, to the year she went home with him as his bride. Then she thought of their growing coldness, of how they found it hard before long to talk to each other about anything that mattered. And how they fought! Then a growing number of affairs filled the emptiness.

Even as she wondered why he had brought all of that up, something inside of her began to give way. This man didn't sound pompous and judgmental like so many other religious teachers she'd heard. He sounded more like a doctor making a diagnosis: Here's your trouble. If you want life, you'll have to deal with this. The life you want may be personal, but it can never be private. Go get the person nearest to you. Water—especially spiritual water—gets terribly polluted when we try to hoard and store it.

The woman responded, "Our fathers worshipped on this mountain, but you Jews say that the temple where God ought to be worshipped is in Jerusalem." She did what I've seen myself do a hundred times—change the subject and start talking religion. It's a little liturgical side-step that's generally pretty safe. When the Spirit of God gets beneath the surface and begins to deal with me where I hurt, it's easier to talk religion. It's supposed to bring me to God, but very often it remains the one thing standing between us. I've seen people get terribly interested in religion, even in the Bible itself, in order to avoid facing the real problems of their lives. I've seen them get excited about minor details—a cross to wear in the lapel, a Bible to carry around, or a St. Christopher medal on the dashboard.

I hear Jesus saying, Okay, if you want to talk religion, that's fine. Just remember this: God is a Spirit, and those who worship him must worship him in spirit and in truth. The technicalities make very little difference. You and I stand before a living God. How do you feel in his presence?

She answered, I know that when Messiah comes he will give us answers to all those kinds of questions. In a last desperate effort, she tried to put off into the future dealing with the present disruptions in her life. Then Jesus made one of the most dramatic statements in all of the New Testament: "I am he, I who am speaking to you now."

Jesus did not share that with Peter or John or any of the other disciples, but with this Palestinian woman, whose heart began to beat wildly in her chest. She had said that she wanted to become whole and new, but not yet. Sometime in the future when the Messiah comes. And Jesus had answered, He has come. "I am he, I who am speaking to you now." Could this ordinary man she had met by chance, sitting in the blazing sun, tired and thirsty, this man with the same kinds of needs she had, be the Messiah? She had looked for someone or something extraordinary to get her and the world out of a mess. That couldn't be he sitting next to her, asking her to do something for him. She turned quickly, left her water pot by the well, and ran off toward town. "Come and see a man who has told me everything I ever did. Could this be the Messiah?"

I can only imagine how she sounded to them at first, and what they said behind her back as she hurried down the street. But she *did* seem different, as if carried along on the crest of a new enthusiasm. She became disarmingly frank and unshakably determined: You know what I was. Look at me now. Can this be the Christ?

She didn't say she had seen an angel, a political leader, or a great preacher. She did say she found a man in need who brought God beneath the surface of her life. She had begun to feel that none of us chooses the time or place of our conversation with God; he chooses it. So she moved through the streets with her question: Can this be the Christ?

QUESTIONS FOR REFLECTION AND DISCUSSION

1. In what sense, if any, do you see yourself in this story of Jesus and the woman at the well?
2. Do you agree with the statement that we all have the same insides? Would it apply to people as diverse as Richard Nixon and Mother Teresa, Idi Amin and Helen Keller?
3. Does the church look tired and worn out to you? Have you ever felt it needed what you could give?
4. Have you ever experienced confusion in sorting out the immediate necessities of life from its ultimate satisfactions? Do

you think any difference exists between the two? How would you distinguish them?

5. *Have you ever found yourself using religious meetings or conversations as a way of putting off dealing with the present disruptions in your life?*

9. Inside the Frustrations of Life *(5:1–18)*

Maybe some people can say, Life has turned out just as I planned. Everything has gone according to the timetable of my dreams. I know *I* can't. I've experienced the frustration of setting my heart on something and having life deny it.

As a boy, I used to love to put a jigsaw puzzle together. Such a puzzle has a kind of inexorable logic. The only choice for each piece of the puzzle is the right one. If I had the patience and the time, I could solve the puzzle. In life, however, the pieces keep changing shape and slipping out of my hands. Just when I think I have solved the puzzle and begin to feel comfortable with my life, I find a piece that doesn't fit.

I saw a woman at a toy counter examining a mechanical toy. She asked the clerk behind the counter, "Don't you think this is just a little too complicated for a child?"

"Oh no," said the salesman, smiling. "That's an educational toy. It's specially designed to adapt a child to life in the world today. Any way he puts it together it's wrong." Life does have this puzzling way of frustrating my fondest hopes and dearest dreams.

A young man starts out to study medicine, but his father dies and he has to come home to support his mother and younger brother and sister. The university and his dreams of medicine are history. Another young man starts out in business but finds the competition a lot fiercer than he bargained for. Though he struggles to keep up in the race, as the years go by he finds that he doesn't have the same resilience he once had, and he knows he'll never make much of a go of the business. A young woman wants to serve her country overseas in the diplomatic corps, but she ends up in an office in her home town behind a desk. Yes, life has this puzzling way of frustrating hopes and dreams. And how often I feel powerless to do anything about it.

Yet when Jesus came across an old preacher who longed for a new lease on life but thought he had grown too old, Jesus showed him how to be renewed. As Nicodemus talked to Jesus, he saw that his age did not stand between himself and the radiant fulfillment of his life.

Once Jesus sat by a well and talked with a woman caught up in the competitive, compulsive lifestyle of a swinging single. She left the well released and able to begin to live in a beautiful new way.

Then one day Jesus walked through the outpatient ward of an inner-city hospital at Bethesda. As John tells about it, I can feel the grim grayness of the walls, the sickness and the smell of it. One man, a patient for thirty-eight years, caught the eye of Christ. John writes as if he had watched Jesus single this man out. He says Jesus "saw him." How is it to feel oneself searched out by the kindest eyes that have ever looked into a human heart?

Just a few yards away, an underground spring fed a central pool. Local tradition held that every time the pool bubbled, some angel of healing had touched the waters, and the first person in received health. Imagine the pathetically wild and agonizing scramble down to the water. For almost four decades, this man had found himself caught up in all that. Since most people went right on by him, he found himself on the edge of things, an outsider looking in, powerless to do much about it.

I think of the boy born into this world because his

mother and father thought they ought to have a family. They teach him how to speak correctly and how to behave. They send him off to school to learn values that will make him a respectable citizen. Now and then on the weekend he receives a little religious training. After he graduates from high school, he is drafted into the army and almost killed; then he gets his discharge, finishes his education, and begins to work for a large firm. During his thirty years with that firm he falls in love, gets married, raises a family, votes, and pays his taxes. When he dies, he continues to contribute to the economy by employing the skill of an undertaker and taking up space in a graveyard.

When did anybody in this world ever see this person as more than a means to an end? When did he ever see himself as more than that? When did his company, or his neighborhood, or his city government ever get together to serve his deep personal needs? Yes, they allowed him air to breathe, food to eat, and a little sex and creativity. But what had they to say to his frustrations, his deep hunger to feel like somebody of worth? Like this man and like the man Jesus saw in the hospital at Bethesda, lots of people struggle through life feeling forever on the edge of it, never quite in the mainstream.

Jesus stopped when he saw the man in the hospital and asked, "Do you want to recover?" At first that sounds silly, but then I remember how many people I've run into who seem to enjoy misfortune. Some years ago a man traveling by train sat eating his dinner in the elegant dining car. After the main course he said to the waiter, "And for dessert I want plum pudding and coffee." The waiter said, "I'm sorry, Sir, we don't have plum pudding on the menu today."

"Well," the man said, "I ship hundreds of tons of freight on this railroad, and here I am eating in the diner and I can't have what I want for dessert. I'll take it up with the manager."

The steward had overheard the conversation and

called the waiter aside as he went back to the kitchen. "Listen, when we stop at Milwaukee I'll get a plum pudding," he promised. Sure enough, the waiter soon reappeared at the customer's side and said, "I'm happy to tell you that we do have some plum pudding. The chef has been working on the sauce all morning and hopes you'll like it. With it and with the compliments of the company, we'd like to present you with this fifty-year-old brandy." As the waiter stood there, expecting thanks, the customer threw down his napkin, waved his arm in anger, and said, "To hell with it. I'd rather stay mad!"

That's why Jesus asked his question: "Do you want to recover?" Would you rather continue in this dog-eat-dog existence, scrambling and clawing and fighting your way down to the water? Do you want to go on living at the level of the survival of the fittest of the unfit, or do you want to get well? After all, maybe the man didn't want anybody tampering with his life or suggesting that he change his approach. He was weak, yes, but maybe he'd rather stay that way.

Dr. Lawrence LaShan, a prominent Canadian physician, told an interviewer of a patient who, having recently learned that he had a fatal disease and would die in a short time, recovered under new treatment. The man stood ready for discharge from the hospital and turned to LaShan and said, "Doctor, you may not know it, but my biggest problem was not hearing I was going to die but rather what to do with my life now that I've recovered."

I can also share some of the ambiguity behind the man's answer to Jesus. He didn't say *yes* or *no* but began to complain: Look, I've lain here for thirty-eight years. Now you ask me if I want to get well. What do you think? If only I had someone to put me into the pool when the angel troubled the water. If only I had a little more energy I could make it, but every time I try someone beats me to it. For thirty-eight years I've struggled to get there, and you ask me if I want to get well.

How many "if onlys" lie behind the frustrations of life! I've run into people who say, Things would change if only the children would straighten out, or if only we could get our money affairs in order, or if only we could get away for a vacation, or if only this woman would go out of my life, or if only that man would come into it!

The Lord challenges us to live a whole and complete life. We hedge: We would, Lord, if only we were younger, or if only we were older, or if only we were smarter, or if only we had better connections, or if only we were better looking. If only we could add a little of this or subtract a little of that, or change a few circumstances, we'd make it, Lord; I know we would.

Institutions suffer from the same frustration as do individuals. Take our country, for instance. In 1976 we celebrated our bicentennial year—a year when we saluted a country established "with liberty and justice for all." If God asked us if we believed in that ideal, all of us would agree enthusiastically. But a strange kind of ambiguity exists. I would like to plunge into the healing waters of liberty and justice for all, if only we had a little more money in the U.S. Treasury, and if only the struggle for liberty and justice for all didn't make so many people so mad, and if only it wouldn't cost *me* anything, and if only others would work for it as hard as I have.

Churches, too, suffer from that ambiguity. As a member of the Christian church, I want to see it alive with a quality and style and power that I sense God calling it to have. I hear the Lord asking, Art, do you want your church to really be the Church of Jesus Christ? Do you want it whole?

I hear my response: Lord, that church has stood on the corner for thirty years. What do you think? If only we had a little more money in the treasury, and a few more members, and a few more young people. If only the preacher took better care of us, and had a little more humility and fund raising skill and administrative ability. Still, Christ's question presses in on me: Are you sure you want wholeness, or would you rather stay the way you are? Do you really want to get into the mainstream? The answer is yes, if only. . . .

If only I had a couple of friends to help me at the right time. How often I talk to people who have felt the rejection of significant people in their lives at critical times. Children have a wonderful way of making a parent feel something less than human, as though somewhere between the diaper pail and the first dance parenthood had been decreed an offense against humanity. The young person may not leave home, he simply pays no attention to what adults think or feel—he ignores them.

On the other hand, I've talked to many young people who have felt neglected by their parents. I don't mean that the parents left the child on a doorstep or threw him out of the house at young adulthood. It's that the young person often doesn't feel included. No one listens to his opinions. After all, what parents can listen to their children when they have so many important things to tell them about how to live their lives.

Rejection and frustration happen in *all* our lives. It's how we react to it that's critical. I've noticed that most people tend to do one of two things. Some get mad, like the man in the railroad car. They'd rather bemoan the status quo than change anything about themselves, so they quit their job, or break up the home, or start a fight.

Other people find situations so frustrating that they just give up. They tell me, I've put my whole self into this project. I've given it the best years of my life, and no one appreciates me or what I've tried to do or think. What's the use?

In the middle of all these human complaints, Jesus says to us, Come on, take up your bed and walk. You don't have to go through life full of anger and frustration. It just looks that way to you. You don't have to continue trying to win this mad scramble to get down to the pool first. The forces of healing aren't somewhere else or sometime off in the future. They're right now and right here. You will find them in the middle of your own particular frustrating circumstances. Your full participation in God's world and God's purpose does not depend on a little bit more of this or a little bit less of that. It does not depend on your being in some other place or living at some other time. Right now, where you are, you can take up your bed and walk. Everything depends on your willingness to take hold of this moment and rise to this occasion. You believe what you do more than you do what you believe. Take up your bed! Walk! God will strengthen you to do it.

Jesus did in Bethesda what he so often does. He asked the man to do precisely what the man found impossible. How often today he brings me face to face with the one thing that seems insuperable. This man felt something stirring in his mind and in his heart, and as he tried to get up, he discovered he had the strength to do it. In a blinding flash of glory I see how faith works—what faith means. Jesus said, "Rise to your feet," and somewhere in the citadel of that man's soul his will went out to the will of God for him. When those two wills met, a power of transformation stood him on his feet. Those shaky old legs became pillars beneath him.

Personal fulfillment does not lie behind me or in front of me. It is my opportunity here and at this moment. God sees me, believes in me, and has something important for me to do. Knowing that, I can be less apologetic about who and where I am.

For one person, that may mean going out and buying a new suit instead of denying himself one. For another, it may mean he no longer has to buy all kinds of things in order to cover up a basic sense of worthlessness within. God's acceptance of us, and our faith in that acceptance, will bring different people to do different things. But to each of us he says, Get to your feet where you are. Don't complain about your circumstances and frustrations any longer. Stand up; start to walk. The God in whom you believe believes in you, and that's something you can stand on.

Though I'll still have a lot of things to live down and a lot of things to live through, the voice of God encourages me: Art, take up your bed in the middle of your frustrations. That's where you begin to become the whole person you've longed to be. Trust me; I am with you. You can begin to stand and take hold of life as you find it. You don't have to wait until your headache feels better, or until that important call comes. I have a stake in your life, and my hopes and expectations for you do not depend upon your reaching healing water. You can live right now by the power of God. Take up your bed. Walk!

QUESTIONS FOR REFLECTION AND DISCUSSION

1. When it comes to realizing your hopes and dreams, do you ever feel like "an outsider looking in"?
2. Have you ever met people who would rather endure pain than make necessary changes in their behavior?
3. Can you identify any facet of your life that would be better "if only" some particular circumstances would change?
4. Do you think it's possible for you to find fulfillment in life right in your present circumstances?

10. Hungry for What?
(6:1–21)

John tells us a story about what he calls a "mighty work." I try to listen without suspending my critical faculties as John describes Jesus' response to human hunger.

For a long time the Gospel meant to me written words —if not in the Bible then in a creed. The Gospel meant theological propositions I had learned or heard preachers lay out in sermons. As such, the Gospel has reached many people, including intellectuals like T.S. Eliot, Malcolm Muggeridge, Dorothy L. Sayers, and C.S. Lewis. Such people say that the sheer truth of the Christian faith compared to rival philosophies persuaded them.

That doesn't work for everybody, however. The more I read the Bible, the more I see how it points to nonverbal ways in which God touches human life. The prophets often did not use words to speak for God; they did something. Jeremiah went about in chains with a wooden yoke around his neck. Dressed like that, he walked right through the government offices and into the palace of the king. He didn't say a word, but everybody knew what he meant. They didn't like what they saw, but they understood. So I try to hear what God has to say to me through John's description of what Jesus did.

First the facts. With an economy of words, John's simple story is vivid in detail. Jesus saw a great hungry crowd and said to Philip, "Where are we to buy bread to feed these people?" I like John's human touch. It's the only place in the New Testament where Jesus asks for advice. And what did Philip say? Like any good committee member he looked at the situation and answered, Lord, 200 dollars just won't do it. We don't have enough money for this many people. The situation is bigger than the both of us; there's nothing we can do. Philip simply did not see in Jesus any resource that went beyond what he could feel and touch.

Jesus then exhibited a bit of everyday common sense when he said, "Make the people sit down." I remember watching on television that wild scramble for food when the Hearst family distributed food in response to the demand of kidnappers. I now know exactly why Jesus said, "Make them sit down."

Andrew came forward with that anonymous boy and his five barley loaves and two pickled fish. The story then describes what Jesus did, but not *how* he did it. John simply says, "Then Jesus took the loaves, gave thanks, and distributed them to the people as they sat there. He did the same with the fishes, and they had as much as they wanted." The story does not say that Jesus murmured a magic phrase and suddenly a great mound of food appeared—enough to feed five thousand. The disciples simply distributed what they had, and it was enough. The story ends with the cleanup, and with twelve full baskets left over.

John's story reads like the report of people who actually saw something happen. Only this story appears in all four of the Gospels, and I wonder why. Having heard the facts, I want to discover what really went on beneath the surface, and I discover that, once again, things are not as simple as they seem. The New Testament keeps leading me down strange pathways into a broader and bigger vision of Jesus.

Here I see him confronting human hunger—hunger that went beyond any known resource. I see him put that human need at the center of his attention, and I watch him accept responsibility for it. "Where are we to buy bread to feed these people?" With that question Jesus continues to place hunger at the center of the attention of the human race. How much simpler it would be if only we could lock Jesus up in the New Testament, to be analyzed as a strange Galilean preacher who stirred things up in the first century. We try to do just that, but he has a way of breaking loose and appearing in every generation, particularly in one like ours that likes to keep religion in its place on the shelf. No matter how insensitive I become, Jesus keeps forcing this aching human need to the center of my attention. Art, where can we get enough food? What are you going to do about it?

I've read and heard all kinds of answers to this question. The first is an obvious one—limit population. Those whose answer this is did not grow up in a country where parents see children as their social security and old-age insurance. Indian people, for example, continue to have large families in the hope that one or two of the children out of six or eight will survive; No wonder they stone the birth control dispensary truck as it passes. People can only consider population control when they have reached a certain economic level. Until then it remains a romantic theory.

Others answer Jesus' question basically as Philip did: Lord, the problem is bigger than the both of us. Send them away. A prominent person said not long ago, "Perhaps the time has come just to let people die of starvation and weed out, as Aristotle suggested, those who cannot provide for themselves. It's God's merciful destruction of human life."

I watch closely to see what Jesus did with that sea of hunger spread out on the grass before him. I watch him raise his eyes to heaven and thank God for sharing the gifts of creation with his family. I watch him take in his hands the five loaves and two pickled fish the little boy contributed. I watch while his disciples share an endless supply with the hungry crowd, and I ask myself, Dear God, what does that mean? The whispered answer comes: Art, there's enough, *more* than enough. I have made provision. For a split second I forget all the fancy theology I've read about this story, and try to accept what I hear now. It sounds as if God has supplied enough to sustain his human family on this planet. If that's true, then the problem is not supply but distribution. The fault lies not with God but with us. Yet I ask incredulously, Lord, in the face of the fantastic rise in population and the depletion of this world's resources, do you really mean you have supplied enough? Can I believe that?

Yes, I can. I cannot believe that the Father to whom Jesus taught us to pray for our daily bread would in the end give his human family nothing but stones to die among. I have begun to distrust the dogmatic statistical projections of the prophets of doom that I had accepted so glibly. Yet what can I say to those who *do* die among the stones in the deserts of Africa or in the centers of our cities?

Once again I turn to John's story and hear Jesus ask Philip, "Where are we to buy bread to feed these people?" His haunting question reminds me of a world gone wrong. There *is* enough, but we have mistreated the provisions God has given us—his world, the land we live on, the oceans, the crops, and the technology.

Then John adds, "Jesus knew what he would do," and I'm no longer listening to a story two thousand years old about five thousand people fed. After all, what impact would that event have in light of our staggering problems today? Jesus took that ridiculously insignificant picnic lunch of an anomymous boy, and in his hands it became an essential sacramental element that met a real human need.

Everything in this story points to how Christ got people around him to use their resources responsibly to meet the problem. John does not give any sensational description of how Jesus magically multiplied food. Inside his story, however, I hear God saying, I have made provision, but something has gone wrong in the heart of my human family that I want put right. Your problem is not producing food—you have the technology to do that—it's that somehow the human heart fails to reach out to those people who go hungry. The world does not so much lack provision as it lacks the will to care and share the resources at its disposal.

Of course Jesus did not believe in simplistic solutions to staggering problems, yet he does point out a direction my life can take. What can I do with my few crumbs? Five loaves and two fish aren't much in the face of enormous worldwide need. But if that boy had not shared his lunch, would anybody have eaten?

I don't have much money, but I give what I can to programs that help in direct food relief, developmental projects, and influencing public policy. I have begun to modify my way of living and my eating patterns. Growing up in the 1940s, I didn't feel deprived of meat, but I discovered recently that in those years we Americans each ate about fifty-six pounds of meat per year, compared to the 120 pounds we ate in 1975. There's plenty of room for modification of my consumptive lifestyle, and that's one way of beginning personally to respond to Christ's question, What are you going to do? But it's *just* the beginning. A more complete response requires involvement in matters of public policy.

In this story I see Jesus moved by people's empty stomachs, and I watch him act as if anyone who cares about feeding people will finally touch on personal religion. It looks as if the reverse is also true. A person genuinely concerned about the spiritual development of others will very soon have to confront social problems that debase the spirit. That's the kind of change Christ brings into human experience. The mystic and the activist come together at the center of life. People begin cooperating with God as he shares himself and the provisions with which he so generously stocks the world.

QUESTIONS FOR REFLECTION AND DISCUSSION*

1. *Do you identify with any of the people in this story? The hungry crowd? The disciple Philip? The little boy? If you had been asked, what advice might you have given Jesus in this situation?*

2. *In what sense, if any, does the continuing problem of human hunger affect the way you live and use the resources at your disposal?*

3. *On a planet of limited resources do you think there is enough food for everyone, or has the steady rise in population and the depletion of the world's energy reserves made such faith outmoded?*

4. *How do you feel when efforts to feed hungry people affect public policy and imply criticism of corporate policy? In what sense do you feel "the mystic and the activist come together at the center of life"?*

11. Seen the Light?
(8:12–20)

I've watched people grope their way from the cradle to the grave, unillumined by any light from above, feeling unwanted and unsure. Preoccupied with money making, career making, love making, a friend of mine arrived at the office of a prominent psychiatrist. He poured out his story and ended by saying, "Doctor, I've lost my nerve to go on. Life's just too hectic, too confusing, and too sad."

"I understand what you say," said the doctor. "Many people tell me they feel that way, but I think that with a year of therapy we can help you feel much better."

"How much will that cost me?" my friend asked.

"About sixty dollars a week," came the answer.

Following a pregnant silence my friend said, "Well, doctor, that solves your problem. What about mine?"

Light on life—how often I long for just that. What have I stored in the treasure house of my soul that has any lasting significance? As if in answer to my longings and doubts, I hear John telling this story about Jesus interrupting a great celebration at the temple to announce: "I am the light of the world." In the Gospels of Matthew, Mark, and Luke, Jesus talks about the kingdom of God, but here in John's book Jesus talks about himself. This Gospel tries to clarify who Jesus is. John is not a reporter of facts like Walter Cronkite. Rather, he tries to get me beneath the surface of the events and words of Christ's life so that I can see their significance for myself. Concrete images like light, bread, door, and vine, help me discover what Jesus thought being a Christian means.

Why did Jesus say, "I am the light of the world"? Do you remember the last time you saw the sun rise through the first gray streaks of dawn as its quiet glory began to break up the empire of darkness? Long before the sun appears, you can feel it on the way. Clouds begin to reflect the light, and dull grays give way to silver or red or deep purple. For just a moment all nature seems to stand waiting. Then at just the right moment, that great flaming sun peeks above the horizon and soars into the sky. As it rides out, everything else is dim and faint in contrast to the brightness of its coming.

I think Jesus meant something like that. Before he appeared, here and there in Isaiah, or Jeremiah, or Amos, or Elijah, we caught a glimpse of the coming light. After these first bright hints, and at exactly the right time, the Son appeared. Light shone on people who had lost sight of the center and were off at the edge of life.

I remember moving my aunt from an apartment in Whittier, California, to one in Huntington Beach. As I drove down the freeway to her new home, it seemed the Los Angeles basin had never looked more beautiful. I could see thirty or forty miles in any direction. When we arrived in Huntington Beach, I stepped out on the small balcony of her apartment to admire Catalina Island etched on the evening horizon, the Queen Mary berthed off to the north, and even the off-shore oil drilling islands in the harbor, which looked bearable and almost lovable.

I began to wonder what made it all look so different. Was it my mood? I didn't think so. The approach of spring, with all the flowers and trees in the bud? I didn't think so. Then I understood. It was the light! The whole Los Angeles basin seemed alight on that cloudless, smogless day.

Somehow, the pure light of the sun made the city and its inhabitants look different to me. Even I felt different.

If the light of the sun can do that, what might "the light of the world" do? Greater than the light of a lamp, the light in someone's eye, and even the light of the sun, Jesus declared, "I am the light of the world."

But what does that mean? If I'm to understand greater lights, I have first to know something about lesser ones. I remember how at the beginning, in Genesis, light came before darkness. Light made the existence of everything, including life, possible. All of this starts me to thinking about the sun. I can't stop it from rising in the morning or push it down again so that darkness takes over. I can't change the way it operates. Although I'm not a scientist, I have read that the sun has begun to cool off very slowly. But for all practical purposes, it will continue for my life-time and for a great many more generations as it always has. It rises every morning and sets every evening. You can count on it; it's consistent.

That helps me understand Jesus' statement about the light of the world. That light, too, continues to shine whether I want it to or not, as it has shone since the beginning. At one point in human history, the light rose above the horizon and came into blazing focus in Jesus. Sometimes it burned with fierce intensity, and sometimes it warmed or illuminated, yet in our tumbled, chaotic world its source radiated consistency and integrity and compassion as wide as the sea.

The first followers of Jesus came upon one fact, in the maze of life's confusion, that made life creditable. There flashed across the darkness an insight into God's meaning for the universe and God's meaning for their lives. They'd seen the light! They'd been with Jesus!

In the true light everything begins to look different. The sky is swept clean of dark, obscene horrors. Although nature remains mystifying and sometimes terrifying, it no longer frightens me. I see it now as an expression of God's mind and heart and intent and purpose. As I step out of the darkness into that kind of light, I begin to understand something about myself. The final standard for measuring life is not tangible, measurable, or containable, but spiritual. Furthermore, I do not live in an indifferent, uncaring universe. I am not caught helplessly in the grip of events. I live in a universe that has at its heart a loving God —a God who knows my name. Behind all the mystery I have a great friend who cares how my life gets lived.

The fact that such light shines does not keep me from often being in the dark. Things come between me and the light, and I wonder where the light has gone. Nothing blocks out the light of the world like my confidence in my ability to make all important decisions about my life on my own. Not even the light of the world can penetrate that.

Suppose, for instance, that I own a choice lot overlooking the beach and want to build a house on it. I order all the materials—the studs, the lumber, the pipes, the wiring, the plumbing—and they're all delivered and unloaded on the lot. Then a neighbor sticks his head over the fence and, seeing the commotion, calls "Hey, Art, what are you up to?"

"Well," I say, "I'm going to build a house."

"Oh, that's great," he responds. "Let me see the plans. Who's your architect?"

"I don't have any plans; I didn't hire an architect," I confess. "But I have some ideas of my own."

"That sounds all right," he admits. "Who's your builder?"

"I haven't hired a builder," I say. "I'm kind of a do-it-yourselfer."

He asks, "Have you ever built a house before?"

I concede that I haven't, and add, "I'm just going to take some of this stuff here and kind of put it together and see what comes out."

Only a lunatic would approach building a house that way. Yet on the valuable property of the time given us, I have seen people take God-given materials and slam them together on a moment's whim. They honestly hope that some kind of livable structure will come out of it.

That approach says, I'm going to live like I want to live, live like I feel like living, and to hell with all this sentimental nonsense about looking out for one's brother. Who is this Jesus with his pathetic Gospel of self-sacrifice and brotherly love. Everybody's got to assert himself and his aspirations if he's going to make it in this world. Nothing blocks out the light of God from human experience like that approach to life.

But some of us like dark better than light, which shows us things we don't care to see. Maybe you remember coming home after a vacation of a couple weeks. You arrive late at night, unlock the door, walk in, and turn on the light. Everything looks about the same at first. As you walk past your desk and sweep your fingers over its top, your hand turns a dusty, dirty brown. You look up at the ceiling and see a cobweb. You didn't see any of this before you turned on the lights.

Why do we cling to the darkness? Because there the deviations in our human behavior do not show up. Once we step out into the light, they are exposed. I can only live in the light if I adapt to it by changing some of my attitudes or behavior, and that can upset me. To avoid that, I often run from the light or try to extinguish it.

Suddenly, hammer in hand, nails in my pocket, there at the foot of the cross I stand. I see the issue between light and darkness. Jesus only had to be who he was to be crucified; his innocence made absolutely no difference. And I see myself for who I am—a kind of marginal creature living between the light and the darkness, and having to choose.

Jesus goes on to say, "No follower of mine shall wander in the dark; he shall have the light of life." In that transcendent light that forever evades our analysis and our laboratories and our wisdom, I discover I can do better things, and I begin to walk a little taller. That can happen to anybody you can think of. If a person moves out into the light, he begins to look different to you and to himself, though he remains the same person. You'll still see all his flaws, perhaps more clearly than ever before. But he does look different and feel different, and he may begin to really *be* different.

I sometimes wonder how many people around me are never given half a chance to live in the light. They hardly know where it is, and they don't know how to look for it. Young people, perhaps in our families, have wandered away from church because of a poor church school teacher, and they say they've had enough church to last a lifetime.

There are many others who, like a neighbor who came over to talk one night, have questions about God that confuse them. As my neighbor stood to leave, he said, "You know, I've never heard any of this before. I didn't know where to look, and I didn't know what to think." The fault may have been partly his and partly mine.

A few years ago the British journalist, Malcomb Muggeridge, spoke to the American Society of Newspaper Editors. A newspaper report quoted him as commenting, "I look back on all the yelling down telephones, frenzied tapping out of words, and rushing to the stone with some last minute sensation, the clapperboard's insistence, and all this seems to me increasingly yet another version of Shakespeare's tale of an idiot, full of sound and fury signifying nothing. So, like an old superannuated clown on his last benefit performance, I would like to say something serious. Just that speaking for myself, over the years looking not very assiduously or systematically or learnedly or virtuously, but always looking for a light in a dark time, the only one I have found shone first in Galilee."

QUESTIONS FOR REFLECTION AND DISCUSSION

1. *Can you remember a time within the last month when you had an important decision to make and felt in the dark about*

what to do? What would have helped you most in making
that decision?

2. How reliable a guide are your feelings in making decisions?
How far do you trust them?

3. If you felt that the light of God himself shone on your life,
how would it affect your image of yourself? If you felt such
light shone on the members of your immediate family, would
you see them in "a different light"? What about your boss,
Your church, Your country, the world we live in?

4. Ask yourself where you need the light of Christ at this
moment. What one area of life would you single out?

12. Does Freedom Work? *(8:27–36)*

"You will indeed be free," said Jesus. But does freedom work? A few centuries earlier a young Greek stood thunderstruck in an Athens courtroom as the court found his teacher, the great Socrates, guilty of treason and heresy. Does freedom work? No, thought Plato. You simply can't trust people to govern themselves wisely.

Much later, an American stood at Gettysburg. In a high-pitched voice barely audible to the crowd, he finished a short speech, saying, "The great task before us is that this nation under God shall have a new birth of freedom. That government of the people, by the people, and for the people shall not perish from the earth." Does freedom work? Yes, thought Abraham Lincoln, if one person's freedom does not infringe upon the freedom of another, and if the government of the people recognizes God's authority.

A young lawyer stood confused in Jerusalem. He asked Jesus, "Which is the greatest commandment in the Law?" Jesus answered, "Love the Lord your God with all your heart, with all your soul, with all your mind. . . . Love your neighbor as yourself" (Matt. 22:36–39). Does freedom work? Sometimes, thought Jesus. It depends on the character of the people working at it.

Freedom lies at the heart of the Gospel and at the center of our Christian faith. "If you dwell within the revelation I have brought, you are indeed my disciples; you shall know the truth, and the truth will set you free. . . . In very truth I tell you," Jesus said, "that everyone who commits sin is a slave. The slave has no permanent standing in the household, but the son belongs to it forever. If then the Son sets you free, you will indeed be free."

Freedom also lies at the center of our American ideal. But behind the words of Jesus I hear a voice reminding me that freedom does not mean quite the same thing in the Gospel as it does in political practice. Though parallels exist, the essence remains significantly different.

Jesus so often never quite answered the questions people asked him. Sometime he sounded as if he didn't even get the point. Instead of answering the question, he generally spoke directly to the person who raised it. And he spoke with a freedom not limited by ordinary logical alternatives of reason.

When Jesus spoke of freedom to the tough-minded representatives of his people, it sounded like a denial of much of the civic order they struggled to maintain. Worse yet, it sounded like a denial of much of the best in their religious tradition. Again that voice tells me, Art, you will always find that tension between the freedom spoken of in the Gospel and freedom in political thought. They have certain similarities, but they're on basically different wave lengths. Theology and politics affect each other, but they aren't identical.

So just what did Jesus mean when he said, "If the Son sets you free, you will indeed be free"?

I know a little bit about how lack of freedom feels. I often feel restrained, dragged down, and I know I have physical limitations that hold me back, particularly as I get older. Physically, I am not free to do anything I please.

Living on this planet, I also run certain unavoidable risks. I know that if I get on a bus its brakes might fail and it might take me and everyone else on it careening off the freeway. I also know that if I mingle with people I could pick up the flu. None of us escapes these kinds of limitations to our lives.

In spite of my restrictions, when I hear Jesus say, "You shall know the truth and the truth will set you free," I feel like answering, I *am* free. Born in America I've never been in slavery to anyone. What do you mean by "You will become free"?

"In very truth I tell you," said Jesus, "everyone who commits sin is a slave." I realize he is relating freedom to what goes on inside of me rather than outside. It's as if he knows that, if I can handle what goes on inside of me, chances are I can also handle my surroundings. I feel him taking a long look at my human nature, at that tug-of-war between yes and no, between good and bad. He sees the strength and the tension of it, and what he sees he calls slavery.

What's worse yet, he calls it slavery to sin. I don't hear the word *sin* much in church anymore, though I occasionally come across it elsewhere. A friend of mine found on his hotel table in Ohio a little booklet called *Where to Sin in Cincinnati*. Today sin has a new and exciting sound, and the people who do it seem fascinating. Judging by contemporary literature and the media, the people who *don't* sin are deadly dull, arrogant, and boring.

Jesus calls sin slavery, and I know what he means. How often when I conform to others' standards I find myself living far below my own. I've run into a lot of people doing their level best to look worse than they really are, simply because they don't want to look boring and dull and "out of it." Who wants to look as condescendingly good as many self-appointed guardians of public morality? Far better to look worse. Paul said, "The good which I want to do, I fail to do; but what I do is the wrong which is against my will; and if what I do is against my will, clearly it is no longer I who am the agent but sin that has its lodging in me" (Rom. 7:

19–20). Christ promises to free us from that inner turmoil. Different people experience his liberating power at different points in life.

Guilt remains a stark inner reality that any counselor or psychiatrist will tell you enslaves thousands of people. Its roots grow too deeply into the very fiber of human nature and the morality of the world to be talked away. But Christ promises freedom from precisely that kind of slavery. I can't work it out, I can't talk it out, but I can be liberated.

I read recently of a survey of Lutheran young people that found that three-quarters of those surveyed believed they could get rid of their guilt feelings by trying harder to live a good life. I can't remember Jesus ever saying, Try harder and you'll feel better. I've tried to imagine him that night at dinner when a woman off the streets came in wrapped in a black cloud of guilt, weeping, her tears splashing on his feet. What if, as she dried his feet with her hair, Jesus had simply looked down at her and said, "Try harder, Mary." Surely cynicism would have glazed her eyes. If Jesus *simply* means I should try to be better, then let's face it, he means God himself cannot free or save me—it's up to me to do it on my own. That's not very good news. A lot of us have tried that for years, and life remains far from what it ought to be.

Why did hopeless people crowd around Jesus so? What has kept the movement of Christ going through all these centuries? It's his power to release us from our fears and miseries so we can participate in the glory of living. He doesn't simply release me from the destructive power of the evils that sometimes take me by the throat. The freedom I receive from him empowers me to do freely what people who love God love to do.

Of course that new freedom requires a corresponding inner discipline, or as Jesus said, discipleship. A cat can walk up and down the keys of a piano and make a lot of noise; *music* involves commitment to a higher harmony. Perhaps Jesus meant something like that when he said, "If you dwell within the revelation I have brought, you are indeed my disciples; you shall know the truth, and the truth will set you free."

Some people think they're free when they're merely unbuttoned. Freedom goes beyond simply doing what I feel like doing. Gary, our youngest son, and I put together a number of kites for various kite contests a few years ago. They were strange, wonderful creations, held together with great gobs of masking tape and string, but how they flew! We watched them soar and climb as we let out the string.

Suppose Gary had said, "Dad, look at that kite, look at her climb. We really ought to cut her loose and see what she can do." If we had, the kite would have lost its freedom. The only freedom that means anything to a kite is the freedom to fly. The only freedom that means anything to human beings is the freedom to live out the humanity God built in them. The kind of freedom Jesus talks about comes when some cord, some line, holds me up at a soaring angle. "If then the Son sets you free, you will indeed be free!"

From this perspective it's not as important that I do as much good as possible as that I do what God asks of me. If I do less than that, I get depressed. If, on the other hand, I try to do more than he asks, I become anxious and nervous. So often when I feel troubled, I sit down and ask myself, Art, have you really done what you thought God would have you do in these circumstances, or have you done less, or more? That is how I discover the truth that sets me free; that is how freedom works.

Christ offers me an inner freedom so that I am not enslaved by any man, not even my own worst self. I find myself free to see to it that people living in this country and on this planet receive a greater measure of justice. I can use what influence and power I have to make available a portion of the great wealth of this country and this world, so that all people may have an opportunity for the fullest development of their humanity. "If then the Son sets you free, you will indeed be free."

QUESTIONS FOR REFLECTION AND DISCUSSION

1. *Do you think that any of the social or political liberation movements active in the world today have any relationship to the freedom mentioned by Jesus? If not, why not? If so, why?*
2. *What kind of inner freedom do you feel you need most right now? If you received it, how do you think it would affect your behavior? What kind of new commitments would it involve?*
3. *What parallels, if any, do you see between spiritual and political freedom? Do you think God limits himself to efforts for spiritual freedom, or is he also involved in movements for political freedom?*

13. Through an Open Door (10:7-21)

John went about writing his Gospel quite differently than Matthew, Mark, and Luke did. For one thing, he left out a lot: the story of Jesus' baptism, his temptation, his transfiguration, his institution of the Lord's Supper, his prayers in Gethsemane. John doesn't include a single story Jesus told, and only once, in Jesus' conversation with Nicodemus, does he mention the kingdom of God, which serves as a central theme for Matthew, Mark, and Luke.

All of this means that John wanted to do something more than simply tell the story of Jesus. He wanted to present him in a way that would give us the kind of poise we long for, that would open the door of life to us.

Life finds me continually opening all kinds of doors in hope and closing others in despair. The physical act of opening or shutting a door does not bother me, but the accompanying inner turmoil often does. Sometimes I feel that I suffer from an inferior interior.

At the time our youngest son, Gary, entered college, I remember reading of a letter that President Willis Tate of Southern Methodist University supposedly received from a concerned mother. Her son was about to enter S.M.U. as a freshman. She worried about her boy as he stepped through the door of that campus. In fact, she served notice on President Tate that she would hold him personally responsible for seeing that her boy got the right kind of roommate.

She said she wanted a clean young man to share her son's room—no beard, no beads, and regular baths. The roommate should be a good student, because her son wasn't the smartest person in the world and would need some help. The roommate should go to church regularly; it would set a good example for her son, and he needed that. The roommate shouldn't smoke, drink, take drugs, or use bad language. She added that if possible the roommate should have no interest in girls, because that could lead to trouble. She concluded the letter by saying, "The reason that all of this is so important is that this is the first time my boy has been away from home—except for the three years spent in the Marines."

That mother had a problem. But she did recognize that her son stood on the threshold of one of life's new doors. When we step through such open doors today, we often have to make split-second decisions. Maybe a few years ago people could take a week or month or year to decide what they wanted to do, but today we live in an "instant" world. The door opens, and I find that I have to make a choice right then. In those moments I hope that years of living and the example of others will help me in that choice. Such moments require a secure center from which I can move out into all kinds of perilous situations. So I listen for the voice of God in and through and behind the words of Jesus: "I am the door."

What mystery lies in doors. I never know what waits for me on the other side. Even the door to the most familiar room could open on to a surprise. Repairmen might have come to fix the plumbing while I was gone, for example.

Maybe you can remember sitting in a waiting room watching a door that held particular meaning for you. You may have gone to look for a job, or to put across a deal, or to get some help. You watch the receptionist carelessly going in and out the door that, as far as you're concerned, swings on the hinges of fate. Finally she says, "Mr. Johnson will see you now." As you step up and take hold of the doorknob, you wonder what will have happened by the time you touch it again.

We go through revolving doors, sliding doors, double doors, trap doors, glass doors, opening them in a lot of different ways. Then from beneath the words of Jesus we are reminded that opening a door announces a movement of life—A movement that can have great consequences, that can change or redistribute human forces.

Out in the wilds of Galilee, Jesus and many of those who heard him had seen the keepers of sheep build rough stone corrals topped with large thorn bushes. In the evening, when the shepherd led the sheep into the corral, each one passed beneath his rod to be inspected for thorns or wounds. After treating wounds, he took his cup and gave the sheep a drink, then sent it on into the corral. After each sheep had passed through that process, the shepherd literally became the door. He lay down in the narrow entrance so that no sheep could wander out and get lost, and no wolf could get in.

The Lord says to me, Art, I am that kind of door. I can provide you the safety you long for at the center of your life. Enter and find the poise you need to live in this dangerous world. Trust me, and you'll discover safety in the darkness, and guidance in the light. I will lead you out.

Jesus arrived into a world sunk in pessimism. Caesar could keep the peace on land and he could keep pirates off the seas, but he could not give peace from sorrow, envy, or guilt. When someone greater than Caesar arrived, people began to hear God's great *yes* to all their deepest hopes and to all the promises they had heard of him. Later on, Paul wrote, "I will stay in Ephesus until Pentecost, for a wide door for effective work has opened to me, and there are many adversaries" (1 Cor. 16:9, RSV). It's strange how when *I* get to that point, I often think, Yes, there's a wide open door for effective work, but be-

cause of the many difficulties and troubles I'll pull out!
Then I see that the open door through which I see those
difficulties is none other than God's Christ himself. There
he stands, saying, "I will lead you out."

I like the way Jesus tied the image of the door and of
the good shepherd together. "I am the good shepherd; I
know my own sheep and my sheep know me . . . and I lay
down my life for the sheep."

At the time of the 1970 census, a census taker asked a
woman how many children she had. She began by saying,
"Let's see, there are Sally, Jimmy, Bob. . . ." And the census
taker said, "No, no, don't give me the names, just give me
the numbers."

"But," the woman countered, "they don't have numbers. They have names!" Statistics have a place in church
rolls and in government, but not in the heart of God. I am
not a number, nor are you; each of us has a name.

Indian churchman D. T. Niles, traveling in Northern
India, once noticed a young shepherd boy keeping a huge
flock. He stopped and asked, "How many sheep do you
have?"

"I don't know," answered the boy. "I can't count."

Niles asked him, "How do you know if some of the
sheep haven't wandered off when you get to the place
where you're going to camp at night?"

To his astonishment the boy answered, "I don't know
how many wander off, but I know which ones. I can't
count, but each sheep has a name, and I know their
names."

Seeing a little deeper into the words of Jesus, I realize
that the sheep allow the shepherd to take care of them.
How basic that is. It's one thing for me to love someone;
it's quite another thing for me to allow someone to love
me. As I allow someone to love me I discover freedom and
courage to love in return. Such love demands a willingness
to share the most precious thing we have with each other
—our lives. Not that we necessarily die for each other but

that we openly share the dreams and disappointments that live within us.

Suppose a husband and wife sense things going a little flat between them. Things go on like that for days, weeks, or maybe years, but somewhere they both begin to wonder, Did I make a mistake? Did I marry the right person? Since neither of them can be a neutral observer, each tries listing one thing against the other. Somewhere in the process the question turns itself around and becomes, Maybe I didn't care enough. Suddenly each discovers that he or she is not totally distinct from the other: "bone of his bone," but also boredom of his boredom, lifelessness of his lifelessness.

The same thing goes on between people and God. If I find myself empty, bored, and tired of life, it may be not that God doesn't care but rather that I have not allowed him to care for me. That is, I may not have allowed God to get involved with me at an emotional level. If I don't love another person, that person may wither up and die; if I don't allow myself to be loved, I begin to dry up too.

God is not a theologian, he's our Father, and he's not as interested in correct ideas as he is in us. He says, Follow me. I will lead you out into life. I will save you from becoming obsessed with achieving your own personal salvation and forgetting about the conditions of the rest of the world. I will help you find a faith so profound that it will begin to affect the life of the community in which you live.

Clearly, people trying to follow Jesus do not agree on every issue in the community, but they follow one who has planted deep within them his care for every individual. How much does he care? He cared enough to go out on a limb for us.

QUESTIONS FOR REECTION AND DISCUSSION

1. *Do you sense yourself standing before any open doors?*
2. *I remember an old-time preacher who said, "When one door*

*shuts, another slams in your face!" Where in the last month
has a door closed on you? How did you feel?*

3. *How would you feel if you knew God would not let you get
lost in the shuffle of life? Would it change your attitude about
the doors that life opens to you and closes on you?*

4. *I often find it easier to give a gift than to receive one. Have
you ever found it easier to express love than to receive it?*

14. Inside of Life and Death *(11:1–44)*

Jesus' friend Lazarus died, as sooner or later everybody does. Death's inevitability prompts some people to call life a terminal illness. On my way to see a friend I stop at an intersection for a funeral procession; I pick up the morning paper and read about an airplane missing the end of the runway—life continually confronts me with death.

You may not yet have lost any of your immediate friends, but eventually you will. When it happens, you may feel like a child wondering what it's all about. My father's death last year brought a special kind of loneliness. Suddenly I'm out front, even though I've lived an independent life for years. Someone I've counted on is no longer there. It feels as if someone had reached into my life and torn out part of it.

Why does John tell me this story of the death of Jesus' friend Lazarus? Maybe it's because, when someone dies, the same questions come up. What happened to him? Does he really still exist? Where is he? Has he simply disappeared? Will I ever see him again? What will happen to me now? What happens to me when I come to that moment?

It seems to me that long before death reaches for my body it reaches for my mind and spirit and hopes and dreams. Ten or twenty years ago I sang songs and had high ideals, but—and here I lapse into lyric nostalgia—I've

watched my dreams go down behind the sun and die without a sound. Stars come out so soon, and the day is gone.
Yes, I remember a God who acted in the past. He did great
things in other people's lives, and perhaps even in my
own. Then suddenly life goes into a total eclipse.

John tells us of messengers that came from the home
of Mary and Martha in Bethany, where Jesus often stayed.
Theirs was a home filled with love and quarreling, for
Mary and Martha had different styles of life, but Jesus
loved them both and loved their brother Lazarus.

Martha was a wonderful woman, dependable and de-
voted. I can hardly find anything about her to criticize,
unless it's that there was nothing about her to criticize.
She hated sloppiness and inefficiency and would have
made a competent club president or business executive.
She had a way of making people around her terribly uncomfortable, though. As one teenager described her
mother, "I just wish mother wouldn't use so much time
and energy keeping house and making it so perfect and
waiting on all the rest of us in the family. I wish she had
other interests. I wish she would let us help her, but she
keeps saying, 'It's my duty.' It makes her so irritable, so
tired, that she's hard to live with."

I've noticed people who have the same tendency at
their jobs. People glued to their desks, after everyone else
has left, who say that Somebody has to do these things, yet
don't seem to like doing them.

Many things *do* need doing. Songs need singing, old
wrongs need righting. But Mary—well, Mary had a different style. She, too, was a wonderful person, dreamy but
messy, not much good at cooking meals or keeping house.
Yes, many things need doing, but some things need feeling
and some things need knowing. Mary struggled to grasp
the vision of life Jesus lived and talked about. She wanted
that experience, too. I've run into an increasing number
of people who feel like that today. Some brave, brilliant
agnostics who tossed out a Methodist or Presbyterian or
Episcopalian God a few years ago have now become a

little nervous, sensing that perhaps they have succeeded only in substituting some trivial illusion for a glorious, majestic faith.

What difference did the presence of Jesus make in the home of these two sisters? Did he resolve the tensions between them? Did they fall into each other's arms, and did everything go beautifully from there on? Did his presence guarantee unbroken health and happiness? I can't find any place in the New Testament that says it did.

The arrival of this messenger, all out of breath, indicated misfortune. If everyone had enjoyed good health, no messenger would have come to Jesus. The messenger said, "Lazarus, the man you love, is ill." The name *Lazarus* means "the person God takes care of," yet that's the man who got sick!

Mary and Martha never doubted that Jesus would come at once, on hearing of Lazarus' illness, but he didn't appear. I wonder what went through their minds. What kind of strain did it put on their friendship with him? Why didn't he come? Why didn't he explain? Didn't he care? I have at time felt the same questions. God should see that things go well for those who love him. Why this darkness? Why this absence?

Lazarus died before Jesus finally arrived at in Bethany. Mary stayed at home while Martha ran to meet him. When she saw him, she didn't even say hello. She asked, Where where you when we needed you? If you'd come, my brother would not have died. What's the matter with you? Don't you care about us? Or was this simply too big for you? If you'd been here.

Once again, John has drawn me beneath the surface of my own life. How often have I cried, If only you had been here! I would like to get my hands on the God who, having set things up in this world, allows death and misery to exist. Yet I realize that God must sometimes plunge us into a sea of uncertainty before we come to terms with life or death.

My view of death, which depends on a number of

things, greatly affects how I see my life. How I perceive death depends first of all on my age. As a boy, death seemed far, far away—almost out of sight. I remember when I was thirteen a telegram coming to our house in Berkeley, California, from South Dakota, saying my grandfather had died. I felt sad, but I didn't dream *I'd* ever die. Only old people died, and my grandfather had been old.

As I grew older and some of my friends died, death seemed closer. A young man I rowed with at the University of California died, as did seminary classmates and people my own age in congregations I served. Because they were my age, I could identify with their death. I know that, when I reach old age, my death will be there waiting, perhaps just around the corner, though then, as now, I will try to think it isn't. Behind all the make-believe and pretense, however, death *does* wait for me.

I love the story told to me by a fireman friend. One day the bell rang at the firehouse, and my friend and his crew, who also served as paramedics, headed for downtown. Arriving at an apartment building, they found an old woman struggling for breath, and they revived her just as the ambulance arrived to take her to the hospital. By this time everyone in the apartment house had gathered to see what had happened.

The men were back at the firehouse for no more than ten minutes when the bell rang again, calling them to the same apartment house but a different apartment. This time they found an old man fighting for his life. Working feverishly, they stabilized him and got him onto a stretcher. This time, the whole neighborhood had turned out to watch as the firemen put the old man into the ambulance and sent him off to the hospital. As the people finally dispersed and the crew got back into the truck, my friend took a last look around. He saw another elderly gentleman coming down the sidewalk with a cane, tottering and muttering outloud, "Damndest town I ever saw. Damndest town I ever saw."

The fireman perked up his ears. He went over to the man and inquired, "What do you mean?"

The old man responded, "Damndest town I ever saw. They won't let you die here. You've got to go out of town to die."

The older I grow, the more my certainty of death resembles that of the old man. Whether in town or out of town, I know I will die.

My view of death also depends on the kind of emotional and intellectual world I live in, on the kind of world-view I have. So many people today, conditioned by our scientific methods, see this physical world almost to the exclusion of any other, as though what they can see, touch, and hear, is all there is to the world. I thank God for what science has done to liberate the human mind, body, and even spirit, but science does have a tendency to center our attention almost exclusively on the world we can measure. If you can't see something, you might dream about it, but that dream isn't real. When the curtain comes down to end life's performance, there's no curtain call. A person may live in your memory, he may live in your dreams, but it's over. That's a simple, straightforward explanation, but straightforward explanations are not always the best ones.

When Jesus arrived at the home of his friends, he began to explain to the distraught sisters, "Your brother will rise again." Martha brushed his comment off as a platitude: Sure, he'll rise again on the last day. She'd heard that before, but all that religious talk didn't mean much to her with Lazarus dead and buried in the cave. Jesus groaned and said, "I am the resurrection and I am life. If a man has faith in me, even though he die, he shall come to life; and no one who is alive and has faith shall ever die. Do you believe this?"

Something happened inside of Martha as, behind the words of Jesus, she heard something she had never heard before. The words shot through her like lightning. As a doctor, this man came too late, but he did not seem to have come to pay his last respects. Here stood someone who could do something when faced with death itself, and all the platitudes about immortality and life after life seemed unnecessary. Her legs trembling, her heart beating wildly, Martha got up and ran for Mary, and they all set out for the cemetery. Standing in front of the tomb, Jesus wept. Why? Moved by sympathy, I'm sure, but also by indignation that death should intrude upon the life of God's human family and destroy men's lives and dreams.

I hardly know how to talk about what happened next. It's an expedition into another world. What John wrote continues to embarrass intellectual sophisticates. His words themselves reek of the tomb and explode with a kind of earthiness. Jesus said, "Take away the stone."

Martha countered, "Sir, by now there will be a stench; he has been there four days." Maybe she had second thoughts about having that stinker back! She certainly didn't want Jesus to make a scene—to start something he couldn't finish—or to embarrass her, Mary, and everyone else. For once, the disciples didn't say anything, but they did roll away the stone. Jesus prayed as though he knew what would happen before shouting into the tomb, "Lazarus, come forth." He issued an order to which he expected obedience, and Lazarus shuffled back into the life he'd left behind.

The voice Lazarus heard is the voice I need to hear. Any voice can be decisive, but no man spoke like that before! It is that voice I listen for in and behind the words of this story.

"I am the resurrection and I am life." Behind these words I hear someone saying to me, Art, in the midst of the death of your dreams and of your fondest hopes, I am calling you to life. Come forth.

I have seen people come forth, not from the grave but from spiritual death. People without any spiritual motiva-

tion or incentive, they remind me of a deserted house with
boarded windows and doors, through which not a glimmer
of light penetrates. I have seen such people come to life.
I have seen others living under burdens that would crush
me, who look as if invisible wings carried them along, and
they gather greater strength as they go.

Now I understand that the resurrection and the life go
beyond simply saving my soul for heaven. Jesus certainly
didn't mean anything as narrow or self-centered as that.
As a matter of fact, he once said that seeing to the saving
of my soul is probably the best way to lose it. The surest
way, the *only* way, to gain and keep my soul alive, he said,
is to pour it out with courage and unselfishness. To lose it
—and not be afraid to lose it—that is how I find it. I can't
concentrate on saving my soul, because when I do, I'm not
saved from selfishness; and if I'm not saved from selfishness, I'm not saved in any sense that Jesus would care
about.

Jesus keeps calling people forth to realize the wonder
of having a life to live. Many of us, thinking we're satisfied,
settle for far too little. George Cornell illustrates the point
with an old Hindu fable.

An orphaned tiger cub was adopted by a herd of goats.
They taught the cub to eat like a goat, think like a goat,
act like a goat, and, I suppose, even smell like a goat. One
day a king tiger came along, scattering all the goats but not
this cub, who felt afraid but also unafraid. The king tiger
asked him what he meant by eating like a goat and thinking like a goat and smelling like a goat. The young tiger
only nibbled a little more grass and bleated a bit.

Then the king tiger took the cub over to a pond where
they could see their reflections, side by side. He let him
take a good look and draw his own conclusions. The puz-
zled young tiger saw the resemblance but couldn't understand it, so the king tiger took a piece of raw meat and
threw it at him. The cub recoiled at first, not liking the
smell or taste of it, but he soon began to eat. As he ate,

something inside of him began to change. His blood warmed and very gradually the truth dawned on him. Suddenly he lashed his tail, dug his claws into the ground, raised his head, and let the earth shake with his resounding roar. He knew who he was! For the first time, he began to realize his proper nature.

When I hear the story of Jesus and Mary and Martha and Lazarus, something begins to happen inside of me. "I am the resurrection and the life; he who . . . believes in me shall never die" (RSV). I feel as if I have met the tiger, and I begin to see the true end of my humanity in Christ. I am one of his kind. Though I feel my weakness and timidity, in him I see the splendid possibility of my life.

When death came toward Jesus, he walked straight toward it, straight through it, and on out the other side on Easter morning. He came back not as he was, but as he is. He didn't take away death or even its pain, but he did something far greater: He took away the fear of death. Once death loses the ability to frighten me, it loses its power over me.

Yes, I will die, but because of Jesus Christ I believe in the resurrection of the dead. That victory of one man becomes a victory all of us can participate in. You don't have to, and many don't. No one shares it automatically. But if you want to, you can.

How? I remember the first year the Oakland Raiders won the Super Bowl. I lived in Berkeley, right across the city line from Oakland, and when the team came back to town there was a big celebration. A lot of people who couldn't care less about football got terribly excited. They shared in the victory of a game they had never played in.

In much the same way I share in the victory of somebody else: "And whoever lives and believes in me shall never die." As I look toward the end of life, I see more light than darkness. The God who had a hand in my coming, and who has stood by me while I'm here, will not leave me in my going.

QUESTIONS FOR REFLECTION AND DISCUSSION

1. *A spate of books has been published on the subject of "life after life." Why do you think so many people have a lively interest in this subject? Can you remember when you first started to wonder about it?*

2. *When facing the imminent death of someone close to you, have you ever wondered why God didn't do something to prevent it? Can you describe how you felt in those moments?*

3. *Can you remember the first time you became psychologically aware that you, too, will die someday? What reaction did you have to this realization?*

4. *If you think that Jesus calls people to life today, what evidence do you have for thinking that? What relation, if any, does that have to our dying?*

15. Life and Frustration

(12:12–19)

Palm Sunday. What a day. The sheer excitement of it. There was tension in the air the minute Jesus reached the outskirts of the city, the news about Lazarus having spread like wildfire. Instead of walking into Jerusalem, Jesus climbed dramatically onto the back of a donkey. I had never thought much about that until I heard of a farmer in Iowa who one day rode his donkey down a narrow lane. As he rounded a corner, he came to an apple orchard and, seeing the beautiful apples, reached up to pick a few. Just as he reached up, the donkey bolted out from underneath him and left him hanging onto the limb. At that precise moment the owner of the orchard showed up and said, "Hey, what are you doing up in my tree?"

"Nothing," the farmer answered. "I just fell off my donkey."

It seems there's something behind the words of John. For years I thought Jesus came into town riding like a dignified king at the head of a parade. I pictured the little donkey plodding along down the middle of the road while everybody stood politely at the side applauding and waving palm branches, and Jesus regally acknowledged their cheers.

John notes that Jesus came riding in "mounted on an ass's colt." His words imply that no one had ever ridden this particular donkey before. I remember seeing cowboys trying to ride unbroken horses in rodeos. I can imagine what would happen if you took an animal nobody had ever ridden before, put a full-sized person on its back, and had a few hundred people standing around shouting, yelling, and waving palm branches in the air.

I don't know what happened, of course, but I have an idea that the animal bolted and that Jesus was hard put to slow him down to a trot. His must have been a lively but frustrating ride.

Off they went, and the people let up a great shout. Just when it looked as if Jesus had the donkey under control, some enthusiast waved a palm branch or let out a shout and off they went again, Jesus grabbing desperately for the animal's mane, the crowd whooping excitedly. There was nothing plodding or pompous about this entry into the city. It was the kind of parade that warms one up and makes everyone want to take part.

Hurray! God bless the King of Israel! He'll set things straight. Out of his way!

After all, what good is God if he can't fix things up in a hurry? Jesus had helped all kinds of people. Maybe the ten lepers he had healed stood shouting in the crowd— lonely men who had felt his touch. In their excitement, nine had run off to tell their families without so much as a thank you. Maybe Jairus stood waving his palm branch. How could he ever forget Jesus taking his daughter by the hand and saying, Little girl, get out of bed. Was he in the crowd, his arm around that little girl, his eyes bright and full, shouting for all he was worth?

I feel a part of that crowd myself. I remember times when I wanted to do the right thing but didn't feel strong enough until Jesus came. And I remember times when I felt humiliated and inferior, and Jesus came and helped me hold my head up and taught me to live as a child of God. Something inside of me shouts with enthusiasm; I feel swept off my feet, because suddenly there's life and glory in the air and singing in the streets. I watch the bolting animal and its lurching passenger gallop past me. The rider seems to enjoy the enthusiasm of these hundreds of well-meaning people, yet his faraway look suggests he's anticipating the future. Beneath all his vitality I sense a frustration, not just with the donkey but with the people who shout so enthusiastically.

Beneath all the excitement I can feel the frustration of Christ. He knew he hadn't really made a dent; he hadn't gotten anywhere with them. Did anyone really understand what was going on? What did they expect from him?

He had worked for and talked about a new spirit and a new way of knowing God, but the people who heard him simply got ready for another church service, or another ritual, or another sacrament. When he talked about forgiveness and going a second mile, they began talking about death sentences. When he talked about trust and confidence, his listeners brought up their fears and anxieties. When he talked about a new willingness among people to give of themselves, they demanded their rights.

Maybe you've felt a similar frustration. You pour your life into your children, wanting them to know beauty and to have lives of depth and substance. The harder you try to move your children in that direction, the more they seem to drift off into the shallow waters of triviality, and you can't do anything about it. Or perhaps you try to help someone in trouble, but he builds a wall around himself that's so high and thick that neither you nor anyone else can get through it. Maybe you work tooth and nail to straighten out some family problem. After all, if Christianity isn't about human experience, what in heaven's name *is* it about? The raw material for Christian thinking isn't ideas or dogma but life—birth, childhood, parenthood, death, and love. These make up the substance of our lives, and if God can't help us here, then he's helpless. I know how quickly a home can become a place where everything, including nerves, eventually wears out. Perhaps this time the harder you try to unravel the threads of some relationship, the more tangled they get.

If anybody ever felt such human frustration, Jesus did. As I look back at that mad dash for the city—at all those shouting people and the bobbing rider on the donkey—I sense again the vitality and feel the frustration. Jesus could have said, I'm simply not making it. I haven't persuaded anybody. When I explain things to them, they don't understand. Those who do, don't agree with me. I might as well give it all up and go back into the construction business in Galilee and live a peaceful, comfortable life.

Jesus could have done that, but he didn't. He went right on being the person he had always been, saying the kinds of things he had always said, and trying to get people into the stream of life. He didn't start cutting corners; he went on believing and hoping and praying and trusting as he always had.

That Friday they killed him. With what terrifying consistency that shouting, enthusiastic, singing crowd turned into an angry, sullen mob. In a matter of days their shout became "Crucify!" From one point of view, Jesus looks as if he had failed altogether, yet he was certainly not the kind of failure he would have been had he turned the donkey back toward Galilee. The cross of Jesus stands not for a failure of his faith, but for a failure of other people's faith in him. It is his faith, in spite of our human failure, that continues to move the world.

I hear a voice inside of me saying, Art, you give up too soon. Yes, it looks as if you haven't made a dent, as if everything's going against you. But come stand with me against the tide.

I hesitate: Lord, a person could get killed standing there. I'm in very deep water, but I'm beginning to understand that some failures are ultimately grander than most things we call success.

QUESTIONS FOR REFLECTION AND DISCUSSION

1. Do you remember the last time you felt like cheering at a religious gathering? Have you ever shouted out of sheer enthusiasm for Jesus? Is such enthusiasm out of place today? Did Jesus make a mistake in not trying to control the people's enthusiasm for him on Palm Sunday?

2. Can religious enthusiasm ever cloud a person's understanding of the basic purpose of Christ in the world?

3. What has frustrated you the most in the last ten days? What did you do? Why?

4. Do you agree with the idea that "some failures are ultimately grander than most things we call success"? If you do, what kind of failures might they be?

16. In and Out of Love

(13:31–35)

"As I have loved you, so you are to love one another," said Jesus. What a slippery word he used. People fall in and out of love, but who understands it? Love today is often the problem rather than the solution.

George Bernard Shaw was once quoted in a newspaper interview as saying of the marriage ritual, "When two people are under the influence of the most violent, most insane, most elusive, most transient of passions, they are required to solemnly swear they will remain in that exact, abnormal, exhausting condition continuously until death do them part." No wonder a friend of mine, after several years of such a life, sighed, "If my husband really loved me, he wouldn't have married me." Many marriage contracts amount to little more than a fifty-fifty deal, with emphasis on the bookkeeping. The husband balances his membership in the athletic club against her wardrobe from exclusive shops. They perceive each other as commodities in a very competitive market. If I carry that outlook to its logical conclusion, the slogan for life becomes "every person for himself." In such an environment we discover that the opposite of love is not hate but indifference.

A recent television documentary revealed a tribe of people in New Guinea who base their social behavior on that very principle—indifference. No one expects anyone else to pay any attention to others. If one of them runs out of food and begins to starve, he can expect no help from anybody, not even his mate. Mothers nurse their children for three years and then put them out to fend for themselves, not caring particularly if they live or die. Only the very old can remember a time when anybody in that society felt he ought to lend a hand to anyone else. The people have become apathetic and dull, caring only about their next meal. Yes, the opposite of love *is* indifference, and when people become schooled in indifference, they're well on their way to hell. Who needs any further damnation?

"Love one another; as I have loved you, so you are to love one another." In this case Jesus did not give advice or hold up some lofty ideal; he issued an order. I may be selective in my judgments and in my emotions, but I have no permission from Jesus to be selective in my compassion. He does not invite me to love other people, he tells me to.

Every time I think about the love of God, I feel awkward and beyond my depth. I get up in the pulpit and talk about the height, depth, and boundlessness of God's love, assuring people that God loves both good and bad. I remind my parishioners that my enemies are not necessarily God's enemies and remark that people need this wide-ranging, nonselective compassion more acutely today than ever.

A couple of days later, with such a sermon still fresh on my mind, I'll see a ramshackle old car drive up to the church. Two or three kids poke their heads out of the back window. A man gets out, and I know what he's going to say. He tells me he's on his way to a job somewhere, out of gas, money, and food.

My first instinct is to make a quick exit out the back door. However, before I can get the door open, my conscience rises to say, Art, remember that sermon? Remember what you said about God loving the good and bad people, about the nonrestrictive quality of his love? What

kind of hypocrite are you? That usually stops me, and I go
to the door of my study to let the fellow in. Yet even if I
listen to his story sympathetically and make some arrange-
ment to help him on his way, my conscience won't leave
me alone. It nags, Aha, Art. You copped out. You've just
contributed to this fellow's downfall. He'll just move on
and put the bite on some other church less able to afford
it.

I have to struggle to get hold of the reality behind the
love Christ talks about. The rhetoric of love seems tied to
some faraway place where the distinction between good
and bad is as clear as that between night and day. But it's
seldom that clear in the choices I have to make. Even so,
I'm glad Jesus issued a command rather than suggesting an
ideal—I can act to obey a command. I sense that when
Jesus says *love* he means something that requires a decision. He takes me far beyond an understanding of love as
any warm, pleasant feelings I might fall into accidentally,
those that come from being loved. As long as I stay on the
surface and think of love simply as nice feelings experienced when someone treats me well, I will work at
becoming "lovable." People do this in a variety of ways.

Some of my friends go after success and power because
they think it will make them attractive—lovable. They
develop pleasant manners or an easygoing style for the
same purpose. *Lovable* and *successful* are often almost
synonymous, representing little more than a mixture of
popularity and sex appeal.

When Jesus talked about love he didn't talk about feelings but about choices. I have to make conscious decisions
regarding how I will live in this world. "Men who lived in
the concentration camps," said Victor Frankl in a magazine interview, "can remember the men who walked
through the huts comforting others and giving away their
last piece of bread. They may have been few in number,
but they offered sufficient proof that everything can be
taken from a man but one thing, the last of his freedoms,

to choose his attitude. In any given set of circumstances to choose his way."

Jesus astounded the world by the way he chose to live. Yes, he understood that evil would eventually do him in, but he chose to lend a hand to any person who came across his path, whether deserving or not. Jesus never got tired of doing that.

He didn't ever find it easy, nor do we. Some people hate us even when we try to love them. Others treat us with indifference, and we can choose to treat them the same way. It seems fair, but what terrible migraines it produces. We often take the easy way instead, loving only those who love us.

Jesus tells me I can make a different choice. I can choose to have nonselective compassion, which means deciding to take people seriously. I remember watching a little boy in a restaurant order a hot dog on a bun. His mother added, "Bring him some vegetables." The waitress, talking directly to the boy, said, "Do you want mustard or catsup?" How that boy's face lit up! He turned to his mother and exclaimed: "Mom, she thinks I'm real." The waitress had simply decided to take him seriously.

It's of course much easier to treat a person with indifference than to take him seriously. I used to avoid an argument at all costs when things went wrong. Now I understand that, by avoiding the argument, I treated the other person not with love but with indifference; I didn't take him seriously. Often a good airing of views helps me take myself, as well as the other person, seriously. It helps me love him and it helps me love myself. How much better it is to thrash the whole thing out than for two silent, resentful people to drift along like icebergs.

Yet if Jesus had given us nothing more than a command, people would have put him in a museum long ago. Who needs someone saying, Behave yourself because you ought to behave yourself. People don't build churches on foundations like that. Jesus offers us the same spirit that empowered him to live; he can reproduce his quality of life in us.

I remember reading in *Guideposts* some years ago about Edith Taylor, who received a devastating letter from Okinawa in 1950. Her husband, Carl, wrote to say that he had broken off their marriage by a Mexican divorce and planned to marry a nineteen-year-old Japanese girl, Aiko. Edith, at forty-eight, still loved her husband, so she had a choice. She chose to keep in touch with him and the family that soon followed.

Later Carl wrote, "I'm dying of lung cancer. What will ever become of my wife and daughters?" Edith had to make another decision. After Carl died, she wrote to Aiko and invited her and her daughters to her home in Massachusetts.

I wonder if I could have loved like that. This woman opened her home and her heart. She said, God took one life I dearly loved, but in a sense he has given me three others. Twelve years later she officially adopted Aiko and the children. She could have become bitter and resentful, but she chose to go on loving others as Christ loved her, and gave God a chance to love them through her.

QUESTIONS FOR REFLECTION AND DISCUSSION

1. Do you agree that the opposite of love is not hate but indifference? What happens to you when a significant person in your life ignores you?

2. Can you think of an experience during the last week when you did something "loving" for someone when you didn't feel like doing it? Is the love of God more a matter of choice than of feeling? Don't our feelings affect our choices?

3. Can you think of five people outside of your own family who take you seriously, who really care about you? What makes you think that they do?

4. If you belong to a Christian fellowship, in what sense do you love the people in it? How does that affect your behavior?

17. Finding the Way
(14:1–6)

An evening breeze whispered through the curtained windows. In the fading twilight twelve men strained to capture the words coming to them in that familiar Galilean accent. Even under the best of circumstances, Jesus wasn't easy to understand, but that night he sounded like someone from a different planet—certainly someone on a different wavelength. Finally Thomas, the house skeptic, blurted out, "Lord, we do not know where you are going, so how can we know the way?" Jesus replied, "I am the way."

He didn't say, I will show you the way, or I will point out the way, or I will write down the way. Nor did he say, as Buddha did, Let's look for the way together.

Jesus is not as easy to understand as some people think. I remember a minister friend who sat down to lunch with an instructor in astronomy. They talked about a lot of things, but finally the astronomer said to my friend, "Would you like to know what my religion boils down to?"

"Yes," answered my friend. "I'd be very interested."

The astronomer said, "Well, it boils down to this: Do unto others as you would have them do unto you."

"That's interesting," responded the minister. "Now would you like to know my astronomy?"

"Yes, I would," came the reply.

"It boils down to this: Twinkle, twinkle little star!"

There is depth to Jesus' words, "I am the way." One Christmas my wife and I invited several friends from the greater Los Angeles area to our home for a dinner party. We enclosed a map in the invitation and notes about which routes were preferable. Then we sat back and hoped for the best. That's one way of giving directions. Suppose, however, I had phoned one of our friends and said, "Listen, I'll come by at seven o'clock and bring you to our place." I become his way.

A person trying to go the way of Christ today reminds me of edelweiss trying to survive in the tropics. An edelweiss will do well on alpine slopes, but transplant it to the tropics and it will have a hard time. The climate today—intellectually and psychologically—simply doesn't favor the way of Christ. Often we have to go along to get along, and in a sense that has always been true. The climate of Galilee and Judea scorched Jesus the way the sun scorches a plant, often before it has a chance to bloom.

The way of Christ and the way of modern society don't go easily together. One fine church member said to me, "You know, we like to take long weekends at the lake. After a while we began to wonder whether or not we really needed the church. Now and then we'd feel a little guilty, but life went along as it always had. We didn't fall apart." This man hadn't lost his faith; it just somehow no longer shaped the way he lived.

Consider the family who lives down the street from you. They're congenial and neighborly, they give to the Community Chest, and he rings doorbells for the Heart Fund and the scout drive. You share many of the same basic values, yet your neighbor sees nothing particularly distinctive or urgent about Christ and his way. He's not against it—it's a fine thing for those who seem to need it —but what can faith in Christ do for him that he hasn't already done pretty well for himself?

Ernest Campbell talks about teachable moments. An overweight friend of mine was chided by his doctor, kidded by his friends, and nagged by his wife, but nothing solved his weight problem. He ate what and when he pleased. One day, seated behind his desk, he felt pain tighten like a steel band around his rib cage, and his arm began to get numb. Sweating profusely, he finally slumped over the desk. Frantic minutes later, as my friend lay quietly on the couch, the doctor talked directly and soberly about needed changes in his behavior and diet. My friend listened; he had come to a teachable moment.

Many Zealots in Jesus' time, dissatisfied with fanaticism, had reached a teachable moment; they had discovered that the old ways didn't always work. Political activists had begun looking for a new way when they saw the limitations of political activity. Scholars who had lost their will to translate learning into action felt attracted to the words of Jesus. All of them, arriving at a teachable moment, found themselves on the way.

Those of us who today are drawn to the way of Christ modify our lifestyle as a result, as Christians have done for over two thousand years. Some have gone to extremes by taking vows of poverty and self-denial in monasteries, where they live an undeveloped life.

Jesus didn't do that; he came incarnate. He didn't cater to the flesh, but he didn't castigate it, either. He used his flesh and blood as instruments of his spirit and tools of his mind. Anything that weakened his body weakened him; anything that strengthened his body strengthened him. Following the way of Christ does require modification of lifestyle but not total self-denial.

Many of us also find in Christ a new way to sense standards amid the prevailing relativism of human behavior. When I attended Princeton Theological Seminary, Albert Einstein had a home not far from campus. We used to see him in his study, a single lightbulb hanging from a cord over his desk, or out on Lake Carnegie in a small sailboat.

I don't understand Einstein's theory of relativity fully, but I assume he was right. I've never heard any scientist in my generation question its basic truth. Unfortunately, I have seen people apply his statement about our physical world to the realm of morals and ethics, assuming that morality operates on the same principle of relativity. It's as though they can find no absolute. Such people don't see anything wrong with committing adultery, or lying, or exploiting other people. They might agree that such things are stupid in certain circumstances, but they don't find anything intrinsically wrong with them.

When I hear Jesus saying, "I am the way," I hear him calling me to reconcile two things—the absolute and the relative in his creation. He asks me to know which is which. Whether or not the left side of the street is the wrong side depends upon whether I'm driving in America or in England, but to drive deliberately and carelessly on the wrong side of the street, endangering the lives of other people, is wrong whether I'm driving in San Francisco or in London. Some things are absolute; some things are relative.

Theodore Parker Ferris once posed the following question: What would happen if a growing core of people dared to say that truth is always right and falsehood wrong, that integrity is always right and duplicity wrong, that kindness is always right and cruelty wrong. We must have compassion for people who choose the wrong, but the accuracy of our judgment must come first.

Jesus never had much patience with armchair agnostics—the type who simply baited him with difficult questions—but if someone really wanted the truth, he got more truth from Jesus of Nazareth than he had bargained on. That's exactly what Thomas got in answer to his question "How can we know the way?" There's more truth in Christ's answer than I have yet discovered: "I am the way." I can't think of a higher privilege or a greater urgency than to go that way.

QUESTIONS FOR REFLECTION AND DISCUSSION

1. *If you have begun to discover "the way" in Christ, do you find any situations inhospitable to living that way? What do you do in such situations?*
2. *Can you remember arriving at any teachable moments in your life? What brought them about? Has your way of life changed since then?*
3. *What has your understanding of the way of Christ to do with your lifestyle? Your ethical values? Your political views? Your economic ideas?*
4. *Where do you see the way of Christ leading you in your present circumstances? How do you feel about what you see?*

18. Drawing on a Higher Power *(15:1–17)*

We need to get all we can out of life. Jesus tried to show by analogy how people can improve their lives by drawing on a higher power. On his way from the Upper Room to the Garden of Gethsemane, he turned and said, "I am the real vine and my Father is the gardener."

For hundreds of years, people have found in these words the secret of receiving God's strength. The profound truth behind them helps me discover the difference between living and merely going through the motions—a difference like that between a five dollar bill and a counterfeit.

When Jesus said, "I am the real vine," he meant the whole plant—the roots, branches, leaves, tendrils, and fruit. Life flows through all of these connected parts, which suggests to me that I can never be a private Christian. I am rather a Christian in relationship to others, sharing a common life. Jesus called Andrew and Peter personally, but he did not call them in for a private conference. He called them into the community in which he lived, and only in that community did they discover how they could draw on the power of God. At the Last Supper, when Jesus took the bread and broke it, saying, "This is my body" (Matt. 26:26, RSV), I believe he meant more than just the bread in his hands. "This is my body" also referred to the people around the table, the community that is the *essence* of Christian faith rather than its by-product. While faith remains personal, it can never be private.

Where do I find that kind of fellowship today? Will I find that body, that vine, in Christian churches? A friend said, "Don't make me laugh. It's easier to relate to people at a party or a bar than in church." He had a point. Only a lunatic would pretend that he could drift into a congregation of two hundred to two thousand perfect strangers and feel related to anybody in particular. Who could realistically expect a large congregation to feel like a close-knit community of twenty or thirty?

Through Jesus' analogy he conveyed something terribly difficult to put into words. I see, in his image of the vine, that I am united to anyone who professes loyalty to him. I am given a relationship with others who gather in church. I don't choose friends there as I do at a party; the Lord himself chooses them for me. I hear him saying, Art, here's a friend of mine. You maybe wouldn't choose this kind of person for your friend, but he belongs to me, and because of that he belongs to you. Furthermore, you belong to him. In this Christian church is a bond among people that nothing else on earth has ever matched—an invisible tie making a congregation out of an aggregation of people.

Jesus went on to say, "Every barren branch of mine he cuts away; and every fruiting branch he cleans, to make it more fruitful still." When Jesus spoke of fruit, he reminded his listeners that God looks for a certain quality of life. The vine exists to nurture in us a quality that lets loose the good news of God in the lives of others—a quality that struggles to end starvation, poverty, and any other form of spiritual or physical repression caused by human ignorance and selfishness. When we begin to share God's life, we begin to produce godly fruit.

"No branch," said Jesus, "can bear fruit by itself, but only if it remains united with the vine; no more can you bear fruit, unless you remain united with me." I know I could do a lot of things without Christ: I could run a successful business, I could raise a family, I could even work in the church without him. It's just that, if I did, I would often produce sour fruit or no fruit at all. The vine must do something in me and for me if I am to produce the fruit Jesus speaks of. The vine must draw life and pass it on to me. It's not a matter of trying to accomplish things for God but of allowing God to live in me and produce his life through me, as Christ said he could. What great good news for those of us who live in this age of disillusionment and social disintegration.

Some years ago, Emil Brunner traced the beginning of our present troubles to the early eighteenth century, the so-called Age of Enlightenment. In that moment of high optimism, people felt they had outgrown God. They had the illusion that one could have Christian morality without Christian faith. They thought they could go out and live the way Christ lived without Christ. Why does so much serious concern for justice in society—a concern that has its essence in the mind and heart of Christ—end up so ineffective today? Why does it accomplish so little? I've come to the conclusion that it's because those caught up in these efforts have often lost their contact with the source of life. If the power main goes out, all the electrical gadgets in the kitchen become junk. If I stand up to preach a sermon and God does not speak through it, my words are empty.

How does one discover the secret of drawing on a higher power today? We begin first of all with Jesus himself, because some of the greatest strength in life can be found in other people. So often something mysterious happens between people, as when one candle causes another to burst into flame. Sometimes a person walks into a room and, before he says a word, faces light up. Off by myself I'm a dead sea, but when someone else comes along, the buoyancy of his life supports me. That's what I discover in Christ.

What Jesus said has a powerful effect on me. He could take profound truths and put them in a basket small enough for me to take home. "Blessed are the pure in heart, for they shall see God" (Matt. 5:8, RSV)—I enjoy that.

Furthermore, what Jesus *did* also has a powerful effect on me. I like hearing how he fell asleep in the stern of a boat during a great storm at sea. It moves me to hear what he did when they woke him up, how he stood and, with a great gesture of faith, addressed the storm: "Be still." Then he turned to his disciples and said, "Why were you so frightened?" I like the way he did that.

I also like the quiet, powerful way he faced the ulti- mate issues of his life. I watch him set his face like flint to go to Jerusalem and, though this may sound strange, I like the way he died. There was no pettiness, no quibbling, no recrimination, no bitterness, no shouting defiance. In that fine, free way he offered his life.

Of course it goes deeper even than admiration. Jesus invites us to participate in the kind of life he lived. I can find power not only in people but in doing creative things. Sometimes repairing something, making something, set- ting something straight, helping somebody get to his feet —that's the kind of thing Jesus did. As I begin to move in this direction, I discover a new power in my own life.

Jesus described it best as loving one another. By that he didn't mean sentimental attachment, he meant a willing- ness to share our intelligence and skill in grappling with someone else's desperate problem, a willingness to stand beside someone in his feelings of despair and Godforsaken humiliation.

Not long ago, New York City finished refurbishing and rebuilding Yankee Stadium, the house that Ruth built. I never saw Babe Ruth play, but I've read a little about him and watched him in a few old newsreels. I've seen just enough to catch the majesty and grace and rhythm and power and timing of his swing.

Like every ball player, when he reached forty Ruth became an old person, and the Yankees traded him to the Boston Braves. In one of Ruth's last games, the Braves played the Cincinnati Reds in Cincinnati. A big crowd came out to see Ruth, who, even in his declining years, was still the Babe. He didn't do well in the game, dropping two balls, making two bad throws, and letting in five runs for the Reds. When the game ended, he walked toward the dugout with his head down. The great crowd of fans who once had cheered him now began to boo and jeer. As the old ball player neared the dugout, a young boy jumped over the rail and ran onto the field, throwing his arms around the knees of this big man he admired. Ruth looked down at the boy, lifted him up, and gave him a big hug. Then he knelt down on the ground, tousled the boy's hair, took his hand, and the two of them walked off the field together.

A profound silence settled over the whole stadium as people saw the affection of a small boy for a man in his moment of humiliation and despair. All the thoughtlessness and cruelty they had felt a few minutes earlier began to fade.

That's why Jesus told us to love each other. There's enough power in love to dispel the cruelty and thoughtlessness of life and to restore to us the joy of living.

QUESTIONS FOR REFLECTION AND DISCUSSION

1. How do you feel about the statement "While faith remains personal it can never be private"? How would you interpret such a statement to a thirteen-year-old? Do you see anything in such a statement that might go beyond simply giving a verbal witness to your faith?

2. In what sense, if any, do you think the relationships in a family resemble the relationships of people in a church congregation?

3. What kind of power do you see in the life of Jesus Christ? If

such power got loose in your life, what do you think you
would do in the next three or four days?

4. Can you remember witnessing an instance of the power of
love at work in the last four weeks? How did it affect you?

19. When Faith Goes Public (19:38–42)

Most people don't mind talking about religion, unless you want to talk to them about Christianity. My agnostic friends feel no embarrassment in sharing their viewpoint in schools, in offices, and at parties. People feel free to talk about atheism, Buddhism, Islam, Hinduism, and even astrology, but as soon as anyone says, "Jesus Christ" in a reverent way, everyone feels embarrassed. A young man who had just made his first profession of Christian faith was asked a little later over coffee by his pastor, "Will you go public with your Christian profession?" The young man's brows knit in thought, and finally he said softly, "I'd prefer to be 'off the record.'" Why do so many of us feel this way so often?

The Jews had a law requiring that a body not remain on the cross overnight. Who would take the body of Jesus down? Would his family, his friends? I watch to see who will show up in the gathering darkness of that Friday night. No one from his family comes, nor do any of his close friends. Suddenly, out of the shadows, I see two men approaching the cross. They aren't Peter or James or John, but Joseph of Arimathaea and Nicodemus, two Pharisees. Joseph had gone to Pilate to ask for the body of Jesus.

Most people thought Jesus got just what he asked for. They heaved a big sigh of relief and went back to business as usual, but Joseph had liked what he heard as he listened to Jesus. This strange Galilean's personality had captivated him. John describes Joseph as "a disciple of Jesus, but a secret disciple for fear of the Jews." Joseph had a private, personal faith that had not yet gone public. Joseph had a professional reputation to think of and friends he might lose—people who found all the excitement and the power this Galilean brought to life as well as to religion unacceptable. Joseph wanted to feel clean inside and still feel free to do the public kinds of things that make a person unclean. Yes, personally he wanted to see the kingdom of God come, but publicly he had to vote against it. Personally he longed for purity, but publicly he coveted popularity, so he stood on the fringe, "a secret disciple." He tried to live with a foot in both worlds, enjoying neither.

I can share the tension and stress Joseph lived with. There's a strong appeal in public neutrality, in being "a secret disciple." I've seen it work in business affairs: Jones moves too rashly, Smith holds back too cautiously, but I walk down the blessed middle of the road. In politics, one candidate goes too far to the left while the other goes to the extreme right. Once again, I walk down the blessed middle of the road. The publicly neutral person walks above all strife, too wise to get involved in vulgar struggles, too impartial to take sides, too balanced to tip into one camp or the other. This neutral person, blessed with impartial judgment and tact, can soothe and sweeten any clash of temperament.

Such neutrality has another side, however. Anyone can stay neutral so long as nobody challenges his convictions, but, unless a person wants to float aimlessly on the tide of public opinion, sooner or later he has to declare himself publicly. He has to form an opinion; he must come down on one side or the other.

When I choose my side, I do so because I believe it's the right one. Yet if I'm honest and fair, I recognize that others with equal sincerity and conviction may take another stand. When I face a serious issue, the person I have the least time for is the one who refuses to take *any* side—the person who agrees so heartily with everybody that nobody believes him.

Such public neutrality smacks of compromise and moral cowardice. Yes, we need more of the kind of neutrality that avoids irrational judgment, but we need less of the public neutrality that refuses all judgment, dodges all issues, and remains the eternal spectator. A judge sits in a neutral position, weighing without prejudice evidence on one side and the other, yet he also has to pronounce a verdict. What judge could stand up and say, As to the rights and wrongs in this case, I'm entirely neutral. In fact, I'm not sure right and wrong exist. Therefore I shall suspend judgment now and forever.

John tells us that Joseph of Arimathaea could remain neutral no longer; he went to Pilate and publically asked for the body of Jesus. I admire his courage, but I can't help wishing he had had a little more earlier in the game. Suppose this distinguished senator had stood in the Sanhedrin, so aflame with accusation, and told the court what he honestly felt. Suppose he had said: Gentlemen, you can't know how hard it is for me to stand and say what I'm going to say. This is the hardest thing I've ever done. I know how you feel about this young Galilean, that he threatens everything we have worked so hard to build. I shared that feeling, too, but I felt I had no right to condemn him until I had heard him for myself. I listened to him, I watched him, and I began to find in him the same values I find in God. That I have not publicly said so before embarrasses me. But now I can say nothing less. God help me.

Suppose Joseph had dared to stand and say something like that. I don't know what would have happened, but I have an idea that many looking on wistfully from the fringes might have joined him in an open and public loyalty to the truth of God in Christ. The world perishes not for want of clever or talented or well-meaning people but for want of people of public courage and resolution—people who, in devotion to truth, can rise above personal feelings and private ambitions. Joseph had arranged his life so nicely, even to provisions for old age and burial. Why should he risk it all?

Then one Friday, out of a clear blue sky, the shadow of a cross fell across Joseph's garden. In spite of the courage he lacked during the lifetime of Christ, I admire the way he acted when Jesus died. I watch a Pharisee take the limp, broken body down from the cross and wrap it in expensive linens for burial. Why did Joseph do it? In order to understand, I imagine myself standing next to him beneath that cross. I need to see some of the things he saw, since obviously he saw something that made him go public with his faith.

Here at the foot of the cross, I find the ground absolutely level. All kinds of people are gathered together, some listless and bored, others hostile, some brokenhearted. There are the skeptics with their intellectual blocks and empty lives; there are people in mink coats and threadbare jackets. All of them are bent beneath loads of self-pity.

As I look around, I see an old friend standing there—stupidity. I find it wherever people reject the best and choose the worst. Stupidity helped put the chains on Jeremiah, gave Socrates the hemlock, burned John Huss, and assassinated Abraham Lincoln. Stupidity repudiated Woodrow Wilson and gave Adolf Hitler the power to ruin a continent. It killed Medger Evers and Martin Luther King. Supported by small convictions that blind people to greater truth, it led to the crucifixion of the truest, noblest, and best the world has ever known.

Just behind stupidity stands fear, cringing in the presence of new truth, new ideas, new ways, change. People begin to hate what they fear, and to fear what they hate. The measure of their hatred is the measure of their fear. Fear on this particular Friday takes refuge in swords, spears, and a shield. Fear never uses reason; fear uses force. Fear hides behind prejudice, calling it conviction. Fear will not trust anything or anybody.

A step or two away from fear I see cruelty, standing with its hands on its hips. Cruelty pushed the crown of thorns down on the face of Jesus and spit in his eye, and now it laughs. Cruelty started the thoughtless ridicule that ended with blows, swung the hammer that drove the nails. Cruelty sometimes wears the clothes of righteous indignation or masquerades as obedience to authority, but always it's cruelty. It kept the institution of slavery alive, put little children in factories, imprisoned men and women in concentration camps, and forced black people to the back of the bus. Cruelty ignores people.

Now I understand why Joseph of Arimathaea made his private feelings public. With stupidity, fear, and cruelty standing all around, he looked up and saw Jesus, who, led away by his captors, looked for all the world like the master of the situation. Instead of screaming for mercy or shouting for judgment, he asked for the forgiveness of his oppressors. It dawned on Joseph that that's how a real human being looks and acts—free of stupidity and fear and cruelty.

One glimpse of that quiet, loving dignity lifted Joseph out of his fears. He turned to Nicodemus and said, We can't let them take his body and throw it out in Gehenna for the dogs to eat. Look, I have a garden just down the hill, with a new tomb I built for myself. If I can get Pilate's permission, we'll take him there.

Once again I imagine the scene. With the sun hanging low on the horizon, Joseph returns to the place of execution. Most people have gone home, and soldiers work at taking down the bodies of the thieves. Off in the distance stand a few of Christ's close friends, surprised to see Joseph and Nicodemus walk up to Jesus' cross. They hadn't thought Joseph had any interest in him, yet there he stands, and Nicodemus too. Who would believe it—these two strong, influential men publically taking down the body of Jesus and wrapping it with clean linen shrouds. The two of them carry the body down toward Joseph's garden, resting for a minute to catch their breath. Then they carry the body into the tomb. Coming out, they put their shoulders to the great circular stone and strain to roll it across the entrance. As the last rays of twilight fade into darkness, these two men walk away, and I see someone else standing there in the garden—hope. Hope for all who consider themselves "a disciple of Jesus, but a secret disciple for fear."

It seems to me Christ has more friends in this world than we know. Many of them attend our universities, sit in our legislatures, and now and then even visit our churches. Their own closest friends may never guess their secret allegiance, but Christ knows them and owns them. There comes a time to every secret believer when he must declare himself, a time when the fire burning within can no longer be hidden. I can't trace the mechanics of it, but I've seen how often the world's sheer selfishness, stupidity, and cruelty bring a person up short when he stands beneath the cross of Jesus. A power goes to work to lift us above our fears and set us free from lesser loyalties.

John writes, "Now at the place where he had been crucified there was a garden." I sense a new and deep meaning in these words. Remembering how the story of the Bible begins in a garden, thinking of the story of people who lost their God, their garden, and their way, I now hear of another garden. This is a garden where, two days after the crucifixion, somewhere between sunset and dawn, moved new and unseen forces.

QUESTIONS FOR REFLECTION AND DISCUSSION

1. *Do you ever feel uncomfortable expressing your faith in public? Why? Do you want to avoid appearing a "super-Christian"?*
2. *What part should neutrality play in our lives when it comes to*

important issues? How do you feel about the statement "The world perishes not for want of clever or talented or well-meaning people but for want of people of public courage and resolution"?

3. Where, if anyplace, have you seen stupidity, fear, and cruelty putting the truest, noblest, and best "on the cross"? How did you react?

4. Do you think "Christ has more friends in this world than we know"? Have you ever run into such a friend in an unlikely situation?

20. With Just Three Words *(20:1–18)*

Just a few words are sometimes all it takes. One evening my wife and I went with some good friends to our favorite Greek restaurant. The food, the music, and the vitality of the place sent my mind racing back to my undergraduate days to remember what I had learned of Greece. What I remembered was the Battle of Marathon, where a handful of Greeks stood off a host of invaders. When the dust had settled and the air cleared, they sent a runner back to Athens, twenty-six miles behind the lines. As the messenger approached the city, people poured out of shops, out of kitchens, out of fields to follow him—drawn like iron filings to a magnet. When he reached the public square, he had just enough strength to utter three words: "We won. Victory!"

Can you imagine how those three little words changed the emotional climate of that city? A paradigm shift took place as exhilaration and joy drove out anxiety and fear. The city looked just the same, and yet everything was changed!

When I pick up John's Gospel and read, "Early on the Sunday morning, while it was still dark . . .," I feel as if I'm about to hear the kind of word the ancient Athenians heard, the announcement of an event that might basically alter my whole human situation. "Early on the Sunday morning, while it was still dark, Mary of Magdala came to the tomb." The impact the stranger from Galilee had made on her life was as unforgettable, beautiful, and awesome as a cloud lifting.

The name Mary appears many times in the record: Mary of Magdala, Mary who washed the feet of Jesus with her tears and dried them with her hair, Mary who lived with her sister Martha in Bethany, Mary who broke the alabaster jar of ointment over Jesus. Can we or should we identify all these Marys with a single person? If we do, quite a story emerges.

Mary grew up and lived in Magdala, a little, open town on the western shore of the Sea of Galilee. Magdala had the most available and best prostitutes in the territory, and it became a Mecca for soldiers on weekend passes. Though we have no evidence, I imagine something like the following might have happened.

One day a soldier came along, kind and strong. Though he said he'd marry her, her brother Lazarus and sister Martha didn't like the setup at all, and they told her so. Mary would have her way, however, and she married the man from Rome, like a French woman marrying a German officer during World War II. After several months, her husband's detachment moved on, and he left his young bride behind. At the terrible "goodbye," he probably gave her something to remember him by—perhaps a pound of oil spikenard in a beautiful alabaster jar. Weeping as the marching column moved out of sight, Mary clutched that beautiful jar, all she had left of her marriage.

Plenty of people chided her, I told you so, increasing the hurt, sadness, betrayal, and anger in her heart. What difference would anything ever make? What would it matter if she threw her life away? She began to drown her sorrows with abandon, and a lot of other soldiers came and went. "Easy Mary," they called her, and people in town whispered that she had seven devils.

Then one day a man came into her life who didn't ask for anything. He made her feel her best and her worst at the same time. He forgave her, as her family and church had not. His understanding freed her to begin becoming a new person.

One day she saw him stretched out at dinner at a Pharisee's house, and she slipped in behind the couch where he lay to touch his feet. Tears of gratitude fell on him for the new kind of life she had begun to discover.

She joined the others who followed this man up and down Judea and across Galilee. When she returned to Bethany, he even came to her there. One day he told them he'd soon go away, and Mary knew what that meant; she knew all about those hard goodbyes. While Jesus talked, she slipped up to her room for that little alabaster jar of precious spikenard and poured every ounce of it over his feet, breaking the jar to do so. She acted out of gratitude for the break with old ways he had given her.

It happened as Jesus had said. They killed the man who had brought her back from hell, and she stood there watching to the bitter end. I see her early the next Sunday morning. I watch this slender young woman hurrying down the dark, silent street. (It's strange how, at critical moments, when the men ran and hid, the women stood by Jesus. It happened at the cross, and again here at the tomb.) Almost running, she skirts around the bottom of the hill where the three stakes still stand, wondering if the population of the world has simply been decreased by the three people they represent. The first gray streaks of dawn penetrate the darkness, a dog barks in the distance, and the earth trembles beneath her feet, for just an instant, as a room trembles when a strong man shakes himself to get up. She hurries on, grasping the packet of spices she's come to anoint his body with. No more does she hear the sound of his voice or see the light in his eye; his body silenced his soul, and his body is all she has.

Suddenly Mary stops. The great circular stone is not rolled back neatly in its groove but is pushed aside. She struggles to adjust her eyes to the darkness inside the tomb. Her body tenses as she sees he's not there.

What has happened? Where has he gone?

Two questions we ask about anyone who means anything at all to us are Where did he come from? and Where did he go? When I ask those questions, I want to know something more than geography. I know Jesus was born in Bethlehem and grew up in Nazareth, but I'm trying to understand what he thought, what he believed, where he put the emphasis in life.

And where did he go? He came into the world, then disappeared, but to where? To oblivion or the pages of history and the Bible? Will the years finally wash away his footprints from the sands of time? Where did he go?

When my daughter was five or six years old, her pet bird died and she asked, "Daddy, where is he now?" Job, too, asked, "If a man dies, can he live again?" (Job 14:12). I can say he goes down into the ground or goes up in smoke, and in one sense that's true. I can go on to say, He went to be with God; he's gone to heaven. I have to use figurative language to come to grips with the great mysteries of life, and I don't apologize for that. Factual language about Jesus only takes me part way. Yes, I know he came from Nazareth and Galilee, and what I've read about him shows me the most candid person who ever lived. He was a completely human person, who said exactly what he meant and meant exactly what he said. He didn't forgive the people who killed him because he thought he ought to; he simply *did*. I can no more get my hands on that than I can remember the fragrance of a flower, the sound of a bell, or a color in a rainbow. My imagination just doesn't have enough colors in its box to do them justice.

Finding the tomb empty, Mary ran back through the city gates to find Peter and John. Her story tumbled out. "They have taken the Lord out of his tomb, and we do not know where they have laid him." Peter and John set off on a dead run. John arrived at the tomb first and stopped, so Peter went in ahead of him. There he saw the grave clothes, just as they had been wrapped around Jesus. They looked like a stiff gardener's glove from which someone had removed his hand.

Peter and John didn't know what to make of it, nor do we, but they believed. "Until then they had not understood the scripture, which showed that he must rise from the dead."

Exactly what happened remains one of the most mysterious facts in human history. Did it actually happen, or was it simply in the imagination of the people who wrote these stories? Even if it did happen, what difference does it make to me when I suddenly lose my job, or when someone I love is desperately ill, or when my marriage begins to break up and dissolve in my hand?

"So the disciples went home again; but Mary stood at the tomb outside, weeping." Apparently the men didn't stop to talk to her about what had dawned on them. She couldn't stop her tears, as places and events crowded through her mind. In the middle of them all, she pictured that great, strong Galilean, telling his stories, laughing, healing people, working, confounding the arrogant, and raising the dead. Who could forget anything like that!

But we can't live on memories, no matter how beautiful or strong. As the sun crept higher in the sky, she felt someone standing behind her. She turned, and he said, "Why are you weeping?" As with so many questions in the Bible, I hear it addressed to me. "Why are you weeping?" Unless I miss my guess, someone reading this book is married to a person he does not love. "Why are you weeping?" Someone who reads this book has reached the point in life where he knows he won't attain the goal he set out to achieve as a younger person. "Why are you weeping?" Someone reading this lives as a single person and comes home every day to an empty, lonely room. All of us have days when nothing goes right: milk spilled on the breakfast table, an unplanned argument, an undone plan. When the day limps to its end, we're glad to fall into bed and be done with it. "Why are you weeping?"

At a far deeper level, some of us long for the profound relationship with God that seems forever to elude us. We attend church but somehow live as if history had skipped the days between Good Friday and the Monday following Easter. We live as though no great God guided this world in which we struggle to survive.

"Why are you weeping?" Who is it you're looking for? Mary said, in effect, I'm looking for a friend who died last Friday. It's not a bad answer, but it's hardly an adequate one. If I'm just looking for a teacher who died two thousand years ago, someone who gave a little moral guidance, why not choose Socrates or Buddha? If Jesus left only teachings, that's not really good news, it's simply the Sunday supplement.

Thinking she was talking to the gardener, Mary said, Sir, I'm looking for this dead teacher. If you have taken his body away, where did you put it?

"Mary!" Her name hung in the air. Sometimes someone speaks my name with an inflection and tone that let loose a flood of life and memory, as Jesus did Mary's. In calling her name, he gave back the life and love and glory she thought she had lost.

One word, *Mary,* changed everything. That's a mystery I have trouble describing, but Jesus never claimed to clear up the great mysteries of life. He always seemed more interested in changing reality than in explaining it. I remember someone asking a church member if he believed that Jesus changed the water into wine at Cana-in-Galilee. "Well, I don't know about that," he answered. "But in my house he changed gin into furniture, and that's miracle enough for me."

I hear someone calling my name, too, and asking what I'm looking for. Someone calls, "Art!" and I'd know the voice anywhere. Mary didn't find Jesus; Jesus found Mary. I don't find Jesus; he finds me. The gospel isn't seeking and finding but sought and found. God left the tomb and went out into the garden and the streets of life; he went into homes and into senate chambers and into hospital rooms, always on the move toward us.

Mary cried, "Rabbuni!" (Hebrew for "My Master"). I can imagine how her feet flew as she left the garden to tell the disciples her news: "I have seen the Lord!" To see him means to understand that I haven't plumbed all the resources of the world when I come to the end of human wisdom and human energy. It means that when good men die, confounding science, when integrity and love seem out of date, that is not the end. "I have seen the Lord!" There's more to life than meets the eye. I live not in a closed, self-contained universe but in one through which the winds of eternity blow. The world remains much the same, full of cynicism, unemployment, and poverty, but I can begin to see these facts with a new intensity and understanding. I can see beyond people's need for charity to their need for equity.

One glimpse of the Lord and I begin to smile at some of the things that made me lose my nerve before, and to fear things I once thought harmless. I can't explain that glimpse to you except to say it's the difference between reading a book on sailing and sailing a boat yourself, or the difference between sitting in the bleachers at a ball game and playing the game on the field.

Without a lot of argument and with no emotion to speak of, during college my religion changed from something learned into an inner experience of a God who lives and frees my spirit. Over the years I've analyzed and criticized my religion, and I've had to throw out some of the things I used to think. I've had my understanding of Christ bombarded by doubts that grew out of studying philosophy, psychology, and history. I've gone through emotional pressures I never dreamed of as a youth of nineteen or twenty. Through it all I've felt God holding me together and holding me up. It's not my hold on him but his hold on me that's mattered most these last several years.

QUESTIONS FOR REFLECTION AND DISCUSSION

1. *Have you ever been in a situation when just a few words dramatically changed the emotional climate? Has anything in your life changed as a result? How long did the feeling last?*
2. *Where did Jesus go? How do you feel about this story in John about what happened after Jesus died? What do you make of it? What difference does it make to you this week?*
3. *What things trouble you now? Can you talk about them? Who or what are you looking for?*
4. *How would you describe your own psychological involvement with God?*

21. I'll Believe It When I See It *(20:19–31)*

The sound of the hammer echoed across the valley as soldiers drove the iron spikes. Where was God when Jesus died? Was he asleep, off on vacation? Thomas, one of the twelve, didn't believe Jesus deserved what he got, but he did believe Jesus had died, and with him died some of Thomas's greatest hopes and highest ideals.

The crucifixion of Jesus hadn't made sense to Thomas, but it made more sense than the wild stories Peter, Andrew, and the rest had tried to tell him. They said, "We have seen the Lord," but who in his right mind could believe that? Thomas reminds me of a boy from the country who sat down to a very formal dinner. Somewhere in the middle of the main course he put a huge piece of hot potato in his mouth. He embarrassed everyone at the table by putting his hand to his mouth, spitting out the hot potato, and laying it on his plate. He looked up calmly and said, "You know, some fools would have swallowed that."

Thomas couldn't swallow what the others told him. He knew that blind belief could lead to superstition and prejudice. Simply accepting as true an often-heard idea lends respectability to great inhumanity and injustice, and Thomas wanted no part of that. Great people have often stood up in the face of some popular idea and said, I doubt that.

Real truth can stand clear-eyed investigation. Not long

ago, some lawyers in Chicago met to see if they could find a way to offer legal assistance to the poor, but the longer they talked, the more they discovered serious doubts about the way the legal system in their area functioned. Their honest doubt served as a doorway through which they stepped into a larger understanding of the truth.

When all Thomas's friends began to tell him what they believed about Jesus, he dared to say, I doubt that. He hadn't gone to church on the morning in question, and when he arrived that evening, he found the rest of the disciples ecstatic. "We have seen the Lord," they told him. He found their emotion and joy unconvincing; it failed to cheer him up at all. He said, "Unless I see the mark of the nails on his hands, unless I put my finger into the place where the nails were, and my hand into his side, I will not believe it." He *wanted* to believe but not without proof. He knew that people who believe are not always as good as those who don't believe, but it seemed to him that they were in touch with more power, so he left himself open to doubt his doubts.

In Thomas I see a lot of my friends, some of whom belong to the church, some of whom don't. They have trouble believing things others believe about many of the great teachings of historical Christianity. They say, in effect, I'll believe it when I see it.

Normally, Jesus did not give the time of day to people who said I'll believe it when I see it. The Pharisees always said something like that, and Jesus never gave in to them. Herod said, Show me something. Do something I can see, and I'll believe, but Jesus gave him no physical sign. He *did* give one to Thomas, however. A week after Jesus appeared to the disciples, Thomas went to church, and Christ made a second appearance, I can only assume for Thomas's benefit. Only the two of them said anything during the service, but Jesus showed Thomas enough evidence to convince him. He fell at Christ's feet, saying, "My Lord and my God!"

Why did Jesus do it, and what difference does it make today? Why should he have done this for Thomas and not for Herod or the Pharisees? Thomas was a person who would not accept anything on someone else's say-so. He refused to clench his fist, shut his eyes, grit his teeth, and say, Peter, I believe it because you say it's true. He simply could not do that. He wanted firsthand experience and time to think things through for himself.

That's not as easy as it sounds. After all, I started my life on borrowed foundations. My parents fed me, clothed me, put a roof over my head and money in my pocket. They gave me the things they thought I needed to survive.

Even my thought is based on foundations built by others. My parents gave me their ideas and their values, as did my teachers, my university and seminary professors, my senators and congressmen, and several presidents. For years I had faith in their ideas.

For the first time in adolescence, and then at recurring intervals of seven to ten years, I began to reexamine the ideas I had received and to test these ideas against my own experience. I would ask, Is this true for me? rather than believing something simply because someone I respected had said it. I slowly turned from a secondhand rehearsal of borrowed truth to a firsthand encounter with it, as I began the painful, vulnerable process of trying to think for myself and to become myself. Anybody who has matured to any extent at all has had to go through something like that, because no one can think for anyone else any more than someone can digest for another.

I run into a lot of people who tell me that faith will do for me what it obviously is not doing for them. They tell me I can expect from it a solution to my problems, tensions, anxieties, and even sickness. They tell me that if I concentrate on life's possibilities, on the positive aspects of living, and on the fact that God does miracles, then the rest is easy. Lots of these people have received little visible help in their own lives. I have no reason to believe them, yet if I say so, they look on me as a heretic.

Cornelius Ryan, who observed D-Day in Europe, wrote the best-selling book *The Longest Day*. In a editorial written at the height of America's involvement in Vietnam, he noted, "The total political extension, I suppose, of any republic, particularly ours, is a young man—you might also say a young woman these days—bearing some sort of weapon, fighting for a cause, which they are told is a cause. There is a great difference between being told there is a cause and believing there is a cause. There is the difference between World War II and Vietnam."

Looking at the doubt of Thomas I see that it did not come from the top of his head but from the bottom of his heart. He may have had a depressed outlook on life from the beginning, as some people do. When Jesus said he intended to go to Jerusalem, perhaps Thomas said, Well, let's go with him. He's sure to die there and we'll die with him. Some people get depressed because of their doubts, but it looks to me as though Thomas's doubt grew out of a chronic depression. His doubt came out of a deep despair about life rather than as the conclusion to a logical argument, and Jesus chose this kind of person as one of his closest friends.

I think I see why Christ appeared to Thomas. God will let me resolve my intellectual doubts by myself, but he will come to meet me in the deep despair of my soul. In his heart, Thomas felt that the real sin in human nature lies in an unthinking and insincere acceptance of a mass of ideas about Jesus, and God does not want anyone to accept, or pretend to accept, what he cannot accept.

Thomas had his feet on solid ground. He didn't say, Unless I see and touch, I refuse to believe, as though he could believe anything he liked. He simply said, I just can't believe a thing like that unless I have firsthand experience of it. How do I know the rest of you haven't just seen visions or dreamed dreams? His is not the demand of an atheist; it's the despair of a believer. You've got to have a real God before you can have a real doubt.

Thomas wouldn't pretend one thing and believe another. If he couldn't accept the story Peter and John told, he wouldn't pretend that he did. He *did* keep his mind open to the possibility he could not yet accept. He didn't give up on church but went back the next Sunday.

A lot of people today have simply given up on church, saying it bores them. The struggle to exist can be so preoccupying that God becomes a kind of intrusion, and people get bored with religion partly out of sheer fatique.

The church's human defects are apparent to God and to us. We who belong haven't done what we should have done in the past, and we aren't doing it now, yet those who believe in Jesus meet weekly to share things they can hardly put into words.

Struggling for faith, Thomas came back to the church, where Christ met him and acknowledged his honesty. All right, Thomas, you want a firsthand experience. Let me prove myself to you. Here, touch my hand and my side. Jesus didn't praise Thomas's disbelief. After all, if Thomas had paid more attention during those three years with Jesus, he might have believed the story, but Jesus would have praised Thomas less if he had pretended to believe something that he really didn't—if he had tried to fool the rest of the disciples or, worse yet, to fool himself.

Someday you may have a faith as strong as Peter's or John's, but maybe not today. Today you may have to join Thomas in his pilgrimage. So much of what goes on under the name of Christendom reeks to high heaven of pretense; God knows that and doesn't say, Shut your eyes. Stop asking questions. Take a deep breath and believe blindly. He doesn't make Christian faith into believing what we know is not true.

God believes in people like Thomas enough to confront them personally. He wants the scholar, the scientist who dares to pursue truth wherever it leads, the citizen of the world, the humanist with curiosity and compassion, who hungers and thirsts for meaning in a life that goes beyond the narrow scope of his understanding.

It does me no good to get all the things I ought to believe out of the cupboard of my mind and pretend with all my might that I believe them. Would that impress God? No, I need to use what faith I have.

A person may have to say, Dear God, you know what a hard time I have believing. In fact, often I barely believe at all. You know that I haven't lived up to what I do believe, weak as that is, and of all the truth you have given me, you know how little so much of it means to me. And yet, dear God, you have not let me disbelieve altogether. If I said I did, I would be an ungrateful liar. I do believe you came to us in Jesus, in a way I cannot fathom. (I don't pretend to know how all that works.) I trust you in your time to give me greater insight, but today the faith you have given me is enough. I trust you, content to know that my faith is the presence and the action of your very spirit in my life. I'll leave the rest to to you, because I believe you will not let me fall.

I find that my faith, which often seems such a weak link, can support the weight of my whole person. I discover that it holds fast and gives Christ a chance to make himself known in my own experience. Thomas doubted some things and believed others. That's the kind of person who came to a firsthand experience of the Lord.

The Lord knows, after all, our very human struggle with belief and disbelief. He had his own struggle in the Garden of Gethsemane. This strong Son of God, who came to do battle with all the forces of evil that have proved too strong for us, suddenly found the same forces about to conquer him. How could his disgraceful death possibly fulfill God's purpose and set this world straight? He wrestled with that question all night: "Father, if thou art willing, remove this cup from me; nevertheless, not my will, but thine, be done" (Luke 22:42, RSV.) Finally, he left to God what he could not understand and acted on the basis of the truth he did understand.

If someone says, I can't believe all that theology in the Christian creeds, what does he believe? I believe in God, and I believe that Jesus is the best person who ever lived. He's given us the finest teachings the human race ever received.

If you believe just that much, follow him! Make him decisive in your life. If you do, you will come to a time when, like Thomas, you discover the Lord coming to you to lead you into a new dimension of life.

QUESTIONS FOR REFLECTION AND DISCUSSION

1. What things, if any, do you find hard to accept in Christianity? Has doubt ever led you into a larger view of truth? How would you differentiate between doubt and cynicism in your own experience?
2. When is experience the best teacher? When, if ever, is someone else's experience the best teacher?
3. Have you ever found yourself accepting ideas about Jesus that others gave you when you weren't really sure about them? If so, why did you do it? How did you feel about yourself?
4. Are you still open to "doubting your doubts" when you have them?

22. Life's Surprises
(21:1–19)

"Sometime later," says John, "Jesus showed himself to his disciples once again, by the Sea of Tiberias." What a surprise! No one expected that. John tells of some discouraged men, sitting in a boat out in the middle of the lake, who had launched in the afternoon and fished all night. Trained fishermen, they had caught nothing, and toward dawn they sat cold, tired, and empty-handed.

This story gives me a glimpse of the point many of us feel we have come to in our lives. Has your life turned out the way you hoped and thought it might? The last twenty years have certainly surprised me. So many things I thought and planned for didn't happen. I have a lingering feeling that I'm just about ready to get started, and yet I know I'm twice the age of current college graduates not their peer. I know how Peter Drucker felt when he said, "Here I am, fifty-eight years old and I still don't know what I want to be when I grow up."

Life can defeat us in so many surprising ways. The job promotion we plan on and hope for and know we deserve simply doesn't occur. Someone we trust surprisingly and cruelly disappoints us. By the time we don't have to worry about the number of golf balls lost, we can no longer hit them far enough to lose them. Children run from our arms. What do we have to show for it all?

From watching Anthony Quinn play the role of a

newly crowned pope in the movie *The Shoes of the Fisherman.* I remember this encounter and dialog. One night he puts on the cassock of a village priest and goes into a poor section of Rome, where suddenly the door of an apartment bursts open. A man rushes out into the street, almost knocking the pope down. The two men struggle in the dark to recover their footing while mumbling apologies, and then the man catches sight of the cassock and says, "There's a man dying up there. Maybe you can do more for him than I can."

"Well," asks the pope, "Who are you?"

"I'm the doctor," he answers. "They always send for me too late."

The pope goes up to the apartment and sees a man obviously very close to death, alone except for a young nurse. The pope tries to talk to the dying man, but he receives no response. "It's no use, father," says the nurse. "He's too far gone to hear you." When a few minutes later the man dies, the nurse says, "We should go now, father. Neither of us will be welcome now."

"But I'd like to be of some help to the family," says the pope.

"No, we should go," counters the nurse. "They can cope with death. It's only the living that defeats them."

John has an uncanny way of putting his finger on the terms of existence in his Gospel; he shows us the unconditional requirements of living. For all of us who missed the first Easter but long for some contact with the power of that event, John includes this story.

Peter takes center stage, as in almost every drama that occurs in the Gospels. He always has either an acting or a speaking part, though often one in which he lets Jesus down. As a result, we know more about Peter than we know about any of the rest of the people around Jesus. Whenever Jesus told a story nobody understood, Peter asked for an explanation. When everyone wondered how often you ought to forgive someone who troubles you,

Peter asked for an explanation; when Jesus watched a rich young man walk down the road and said, How much difficulty people with money have in entering the kingdom of God, Peter expressed what everyone was thinking: Well, look at us, Lord. We left everything and have come to follow you.

A cool-headed person often thinks twice before he speaks, but Peter rarely did. Outspoken, sensitive, quick-tempered, and enthusiastic, he must have had a boyish expression on his face, a flash in his eye, and a heartiness in his laugh. No wonder Jesus chose such a warm, generous, outgoing person.

So many things surprised Peter as he followed Jesus, yet on the night of Christ's arrest he had the courage to follow the mob into the lion's den, the court of the high priest. Once there, events took him by surprise, and he found himself saying things he had never planned to say and doing things he had never planned to do.

One of the girls serving refreshments to the arresting officers stopped and stared at him. Peter overheard her whisper to some of the group, There's one of them. He was with them.

Peter felt his heart jump into his throat, and he said, before thinking, "Woman, I do not know him" (Luke 22: 57).

Who of us hasn't done that? I myself, suddenly caught in a tight spot, have said things I never thought I'd say— surprising, unexpected things.

That's the difference between Peter and Judas. Judas planned to betray Jesus and did so according to his plan. Peter didn't plan to do any such thing, yet when taken by surprise, he found himself betraying himself as well as his Lord.

Obviously Peter didn't know what to do about the resurrection that followed. How does one handle something like that? In John's story it sounds as if things very quickly went back to normal. After all, with no more great sermons to listen to, no more great crowds to enjoy, what could they do? Three years earlier, Peter had walked down the sands of the Sea of Galilee to follow Jesus, and he now retraced those steps back to his home. He said, I'm going fishing. I can't cope with the surprises life keeps handing me, but I can fish. And John and James agreed. I wonder what Peter's mother-in-law thought when he walked through the door, what the people in the fishing business thought when he launched his boat again. He had gone off so full of enthusiasm to follow this Galilean preacher, and he came back—back to business as usual, as if nothing had happened, or as if what had happened really didn't matter much.

The enemy of God and his surprises is routine. How often I use my daily routine to insulate myself against new things God might want to do in my life. Peter tried to hide in his work from what he couldn't understand and from the mistakes he had made, just as we do.

Peter and the others launched the boat and fished all afternoon and all night in vain. They saw a dim figure on the beach and heard a voice: "Friends, have you caught anything?"

"No," they replied.

"Shoot the net to starboard and you will make a catch." They could have ignored the advice or rowed off in another direction, but they didn't. They shot the net to starboard and found that they couldn't haul the net aboard because of its load of fish. The disciple whom Jesus loved said to Peter, "It is the Lord!" When they got close enough to shore Peter pulled his shirt on and jumped overboard, while the rest of them dragged the boat and the net in. Jesus, who had some bread and a charcoal fire, told them to bring over some of their fish. As they gathered around, not daring to ask who he was, Jesus broke the bread and gave it to them.

They came to shore cold, tired, and discouraged, and Jesus filled their emptiness. It's a beautiful story, but you and I don't live in Galilee, nor is this the first century. What difference does what happened then make now? In what sense, if any, can Christ fill the emptiness of our lives? Though this story doesn't answer my questions directly, I hear God telling me a couple of significant things. He tells me not how I can find Jesus but how Jesus finds me!

Throughout the New Testament accounts of Easter I discover, to my surprise, that nowhere did people go out and look for Jesus. None of them thought they could find him or knew where to look. In every case, including this one, it was Jesus who went looking for them. These men had gone to look for fish not for some religious experience. The Lord appeared when and where they least expected him.

I know that I can't discover in the New Testament a method of praying or meditation whereby I can work myself into the presence of God, but there's good news there. There's a living God loose in the world with my name in his heart and on his lips, and he can find me in the empty routine of life. I believe in him today because he went looking for me and kept looking for me through all my years of confusion. To this day, he simply won't let go of me.

He keeps saying to me, as he said to Peter, Do you love me more than all else? He doesn't ask, Art, do you think you follow me better than most people do? His frighteningly simple query suggests that a questionable loyalty could be dangerous to him and to me. Many highly competent, well-balanced people fall for fantastic, mindless, religious frauds. Why? Because no human spirit can long feel satisfied without some kind of loyalty. If I don't give myself to some great, beautiful loyalty, I'll give myself to some cheap, flashy one. Jesus doesn't settle for admiration or applause; he demands my undivided loyalty.

Like Peter, I shiver a little when I hear God's question. I answer much as he did: Lord, you know everything about me. You know how I feel, how in spite of my inconsistencies and inadequacies I love you. You and others know that I've made mistakes, but I appeal to you, who know I love you.

It's such a surprise to hear Jesus say to Peter, "Feed my sheep." Behind those words I hear him speaking to me: Art, in spite of the mistakes you've made, I still have confidence in you. I know how dark and frustrating the world looks to you. It looks badly battered, but it's not; you can still find joy there. There's the joy of opening the door of life to another person; the joy of losing your life—a little bit of it here, a little bit of it there—and discovering yourself alive in a larger sphere, alive in a way that springs from a little death along the way and the great death at the end. Death is the seed from which life springs. You can discover the power and joy of the resurrection in your life now, and I want you to feed my sheep on it.

And he continues as he spoke to Peter: "Further, I tell you this in very truth: when you were young you fastened your belt around you and walked where you chose; but when you are old you will stretch out your arms, and a stranger will bind you fast, and carry you where you have no wish to go. . . . Follow me."

Those words become the word of God for me. I hear him saying, in effect, Art, in the future a great many things will change, including you, but some things will not change.

The weather changes, the calendar changes, and the map of Europe I studied as a sixth grader changes. Thirty years ago truck farmers grew green beans where our church now stands.

I also change. When a friend comes up to me and says, "Art, you haven't changed a bit," I appreciate it, but I know I only have to pull out an old photograph to be told differently. I don't see things today exactly as I did ten years ago, either—at least I hope I don't.

But the words of Jesus, "Follow me," will not change. I'll continue to follow him in the future as I have tried to follow him in the past, remembering that some things do not change.

My daughter, who graduated recently with an advanced degree in architecture, once shared with me pictures of the Greek Parthenon with its classic straight lines, the Renaissance Basilica of St. Peter's in Rome built eighteen hundred years later, and modern sanctuaries we worship in today. No two of the buildings look alike, but the sense of architectural proportion remains. The actual proportions of the buildings are different, but the *sense* of proportion remains.

Patterns of life change, but certain values remain. Though my ideas and images of God may change, God himself does not. That's what Jesus meant when he said, "Follow me." Centuries ago people had an image of Jesus that doesn't fit my idea of him today. In the Dark Ages and later in the Middle Ages, he was painted on a cross or up in heaven, with his feet rarely touching ground. He seemed out of touch with most common people until the nineteenth century, when people began to see him as a very human being. Our views of Jesus change, yet Jesus remains recognizably the same; he doesn't make new rules but new lives. I can still follow him.

In one sense I have no idea what the future will bring, but I know one thing about it—I *have* a future. God encourages me, saying, Follow me. There's more to come. There's even more of me to come; I'm not simply left to act out my life. God isn't finished with me yet, nor will he ever be. He's in the process of making something out of my life and out of yours: Friend, there's one thing that will not change. In the future you can follow me.

QUESTIONS FOR REFLECTION AND DISCUSSION

1. What kinds of things have surprised you in the last ten years? The last year? The last week? What things have or have not turned out as you hoped?
2. Can you think of a time when you surprised yourself by

saying or doing things you thought you'd never say or do?
What happened as a result?

3. Have you ever experienced the "presence of the Lord" in a
completely irreligious setting? If not, have you heard of
anyone who has? What difference, if any, did it make?

4. Do you see any dangers inherent in a questionable loyalty?

5. What changes, if any, have come about in your life as a result
of your attempts in the last two months to follow Jesus?